Santa Cruz County

An Illustrated History by
Jennie Dennis Verardo and Denzil Verardo, Ph.D.

Partners in Progress by Rick Hamman

Produced in cooperation with the Santa Cruz Area
Chamber of Commerce

Windsor Publications, Inc.
Northridge, California

Restless Paradise
Santa Cruz County

Previous page: The Santa Cruz Lighthouse at Lighthouse Point is a popular spot for viewing the area's spectacular coastline. Courtesy, Alexander Lowry

Right: C.F. Miller's Neptune Baths joined Leibbrandt's Bathhouses as beachfront attractions in Santa Cruz. Horse-drawn streetcars provided early transportation. This photo predates 1906 when horses were banned from the beach. Courtesy, Jennie and Denzil Verardo

Windsor Publications, Inc.—History Books Division

Vice-President/Publishing: Hal Silverman
Editorial Director: Teri Davis Greenberg
Design Director: Alexander D'Anca
Corporate Biography Director: Karen Story

Staff for *Restless Paradise*
Editor: Marilyn Horn
Picture Editors: Laura Cordova, Susan Wells
Assistant Director, Corporate Biographies: Phyllis Gray
Editor, Corporate Biographies: Judith L. Hunter
Production Editor, Corporate Biographies: Una FitzSimons
Editorial Assistants: Brenda Berryhill, Kathy M. Brown, Nina Kanga, Susan
    Kanga, Heather Martin, Pat Pittman, Jeff Reeves
Proofreader: Susan J. Muhler
Art Director: Ellen Ifrah
Designer: Thomas Prager
Layout Artist, Corporate Biographies: Mari Catherine Preimesberger
Sales Representative: Gina Woolf

Library of Congress Cataloging-in-Publication Data

Verardo, Jennie Dennis.
    Santa Cruz County : restless paradise : an illustrated history / by Jennie
Dennis Verardo and Denzil Verardo.—1st ed.
    p. 9 cm.
    "Produced in cooperation with the Santa Cruz Area Chamber of Commerce."
    "Partners in progress, by Rick Hamman": p. 95
    Bibliography: p. 140
    Includes Index.
    ISBN 0-89781-228-X
    1. Santa Cruz County (Calif.)—History. 2. Santa Cruz County (Calif.)—
Description and travel—Views. 3. Santa Cruz County (Calif.)—Industries. I.
Verardo, Denzil. II. Hamman, Rick. 1944-Partners in progress. 1987. III. Title.
F868.S3V47 1987   979.4'71—dc 19   87-25180
                                                            CIP

©1987 Windsor Publications, Inc.
All rights reserved
Published 1987
Printed in the United States
First Edition

CONTENTS

Preface 7

Chapter One **A PUEBLO AND A PIRATE** 9

Chapter Two **REDWOODS TO ROLLER COASTERS** 21

Chapter Three **"AS A CITY UPON A HILL"** 35

Chapter Four **BEYOND THE PUEBLO** 49

Chapter Five **PRIDE, PREJUDICE, AND PROTEST** 73

Chapter Six **PARADISE REVISITED** 85

Chapter Seven **PARTNERS IN PROGRESS** 95

Bibliography 140

Index 143

To Claude A. "Tony" Look,

whose monumental efforts have helped preserve paradise

for generations yet unborn.

PREFACE

Restless Paradise—it is a contradiction which has succeeded in Santa Cruz County.

Santa Cruz County is indeed a "restless paradise." The physical paradise is immediately apparent to even the most critical observer. The restless quality comes both from the surroundings and from the energy and involvement of residents and visitors.

We have not attempted a definitive work on the county but rather a readable, enjoyable, and accurate illustrated history which we hope will appeal to casual readers and to serious historians. These pages will provide a window through which Santa Cruz County's past may be viewed. We have tried to present and explore those qualities of its environment and human nature which have led to the area's unique development.

As with any work of this magnitude, there were many who made the research and writing tasks easier and more enjoyable. Carol Champion, Paul Stubbs, and Rita Bottoms in Special Collections at the UCSC Library were of invaluable assistance. We were extended every research courtesy, as well as being made to feel very much at home. As a public repository for local photographs and research material, there are few comparable to UCSC and none staffed more professionally. Don Fukuda, senior photographer at the UCSC Photo Lab, and his staff are much appreciated for both photo duplication work and for their willingness to work within our deadline requirements.

Mrs. Maeve Devlin, manager of the Holy Cross Church Reliquary, was most gracious in permitting us to photograph the beautiful Trousset painting which became the cover illustration.

At times encouragement is as welcome and needed as research assistance, and Alzora Snyder of the Pajaro Valley Historical Association and Charles Prentiss and Sally Legakis at the Santa Cruz City Museum offered generous portions of both. For that we are grateful.

The Sempervirens Fund of Los Altos provided access to their valuable Santa Cruz County photo files as well as support and encouragement of the project.

There are many others whose assistance was much appreciated: Kirk Smith, Jason Greenlee, Robert Reese, Richard McKillop; the Monterey Bay Natural History Association; Ann Turner, librarian of the Santa Cruz City-County Library System; the staff of the Watsonville Library; Myra Kong, Castroville Branch librarian, Monterey County Library System; the Santa Cruz Historical Trust; Alexander Lowry; and our patient editor, Marilyn Horn.

A special word of appreciation is due for the Santa Cruz Chamber of Commerce without whose sponsorship this work might not have been possible. We also appreciate the endorsements of the Aptos Chamber of Commerce, the Capitola Chamber of Commerce, the San Lorenzo Valley Chamber of Commerce, the Scotts Valley Chamber of Commerce, the Soquel Chamber of Commerce, and the Watsonville Chamber of Commerce and Agriculture.

And last, but by no means least, we thank our valued research assistant (and son), Mark Verardo, who shared our accomplishments and frustrations in the research and preparation of this work.

Jennie and Denzil Verardo
Castroville, California, 1987

The redwoods awe all who gaze at them. Big Basin Redwoods, where this photo was taken, was California's first state park. Courtesy, Alexander Lowry

SANTA CRUZ COUNTY

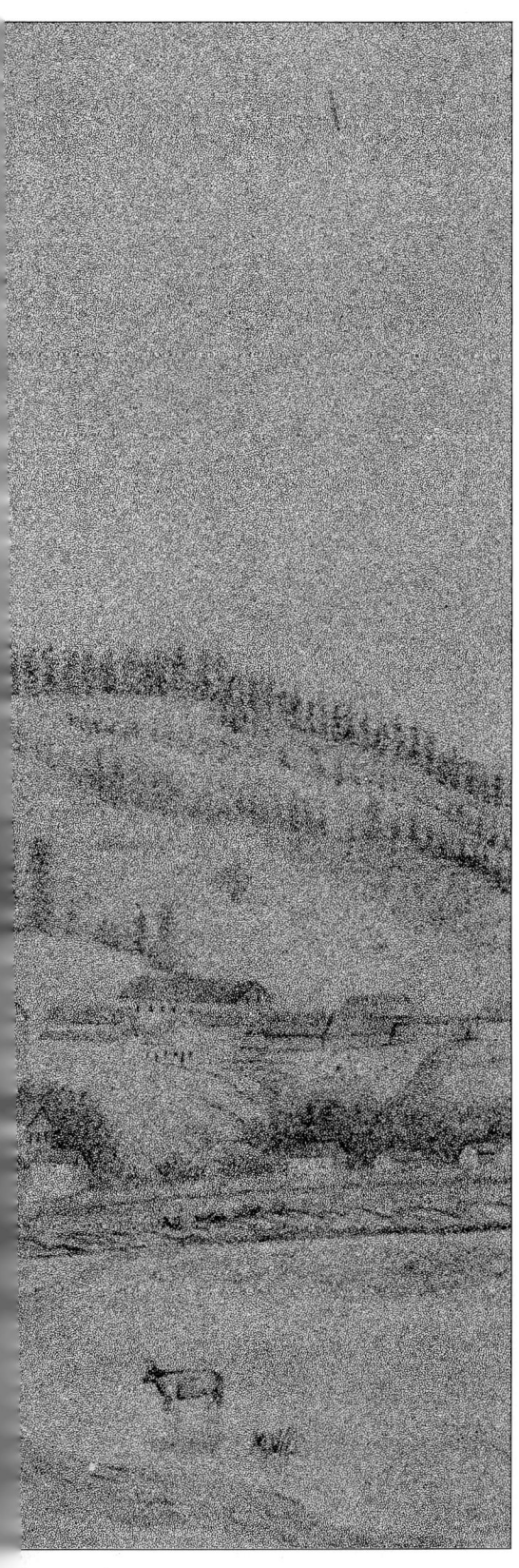

Noted artist Henry Miller sketched this scene of the mission and town of Santa Cruz in 1856. Mission Santa Cruz and the pueblo of Branciforte were so close to each other that numerous conflicts occurred between these two Spanish institutions. Eventually, the two grew together and became incorporated into the city of Santa Cruz. Courtesy, the Bancroft Library

Chapter One

A PUEBLO AND A PIRATE

Although Santa Cruz is California's second smallest county, within its 439 square miles lie uncommon environmental and geographical variety. Bounded by Monterey Bay and the Pacific Ocean on the west and the Santa Cruz Mountains on the east, the county ranges in elevation from sea level to over 3,000 feet. Within its area lie about 40,000 acres of rich bottomlands along its streams and another 50,000 acres of agricultural-quality land extending from the uplifted plateaus along the coast to the timberline. Most of its remaining 200,000 acres are mountainous.

The county's streams and creeks are numerous, with most flowing year-round. Major rivers are the San Lorenzo, which drains its valley through the city of Santa Cruz; and the Pajaro, which forms the boundary with Monterey County and flows beside the city of Watsonville. Annual rainfall in the county ranges from 20 inches in the city of Santa Cruz to over 60 inches a few miles away in the mountains. Due to the county's proximity to the ocean, temperatures remain relatively mild throughout the seasons.

The landforms of Santa Cruz County were created through prehistoric geologic actions of sedimentation, volcanic activity, uplifting, folding, faulting, and erosion. The continuing activity of several

SANTA CRUZ COUNTY

Above: Fire's terrible beauty, pictured here in 1959, is a mostly unwelcomed visitor to Santa Cruz County. The Costanoans, however, used fire as a method of protecting oak trees—valuable to the Indians because of their acorns, an important food source—from the encroachment of brush, as well as a way to increase wild animal grazing areas. Courtesy, Jason Greenlee

Below: Santa Cruz is blessed not only with sandy beaches on Monterey Bay, but also with a scenic restless coastline which was described by the area's earliest explorers. With the invention of the camera, Santa Cruz County's natural arches became a popular subject with photographers, as this 1889 photo illustrates. Courtesy, UCSC Special Collections

A PUEBLO AND A PIRATE

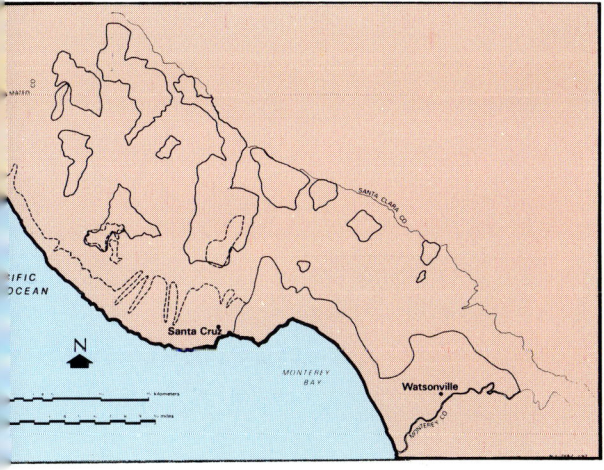

Above: Fire was such an important resource management technique to the Costanoans that virtually all inhabited areas were at one time burned over by them. This 1980 illustration projects the results of 50 years of both Indian burning and natural fires in Santa Cruz County prior to European occupation. The solid lines show where historical evidence for burning exists; the dashed lines show where burning could have occurred. Courtesy, Jason Greenlee

Below: Only about 10 Costanoan baskets are known to exist today. The one shown, collected in 1885 as a relic of Mission Santa Cruz, was once covered with red woodpecker scalps and mallard duck feathers between the rim and the first row of beads. Courtesy, Santa Cruz City Museum & Riverside Museum Press

earthquake faults coupled with continuous erosion make Santa Cruz County geologically active.

Within the restless paradise that is Santa Cruz County, physical features led to a richness of plant and animal life impressive even to the area's earliest explorers. But before European realization of its riches, Central California had for centuries supported one of the highest densities of native Americans on the continent.

With the arrival of the first European explorers, the native inhabitants of Santa Cruz County began to be called Costanoans. The name was derived from *Coastaños,* a Spanish term meaning "coast people," and it described a linguistic grouping of people who actually spoke several related languages. Within the Costanoan culture, there were some 50 separate political groups. The Costanoans actually ranged from the San Francisco Bay region on the north, through the area of Monterey Bay, to well into the Salinas Valley on the south.

The abundance of plant and animal life in the Monterey Bay area offered the Costanoans the opportunity to live probably well above subsistence level. Acorns provided the main source of food, although the Indians also ate seeds, roots, berries, clover, and cattail. Also eaten were birds, deer, bear, fish, rodents, reptiles, skunk, raccoon, rabbits, seals, sea lions, and larger marine mammals such as whales, which occasionally washed ashore. Shellfish formed an additional part of the Costanoan diet.

The Costanoans used fire to practice management of the natural resources. Along the coast, grasslands, oak woodland, and brush were frequently burned, probably to protect valuable oaks from brush encroachment, to increase wild animal grazing areas, and to hunt rabbits. As a result, food and resources were abundant enough to enable the Costanoans to trade with neighboring groups.

The Costanoans were adept basket makers. Their homes were typically dome-shaped structures built of thatched materials. They were also skilled weapon makers. These weapons were used both for hunting and warfare, although a gentle and friendly nature is generally attributed to the Costanoans. The harmony of the Indians' way of life was interrupted by European intrusion.

The land which is today Santa Cruz County was on the fringes of Spain's global empire. In 1542 Juan Rodriquez Cabrillo, a Portuguese navigator sailing for Spain, was the first European to explore the California coast. For the next 50 years, Spain's interest in California was limited to having its richly laden Manila galleons running down the coast on their voyages from the Philippines to Mexico.

By the end of the sixteenth century, Spain recognized that it needed an Upper California port of call both to provision ships and to supply a degree of protection from English privateers who had successfully looted several of the galleons. In 1602 Sebastián Vizcaíno set out from Acapulco to search for an Alta California harbor. On December 16 Vizcaíno entered a bay which he named for the viceroy,

11

the Conde de Monterey. He remained there for several weeks and glowingly described it as "the best port that could be desired, it has many pines . . . and water in great quantity, all near shore." Vizcaíno's navigation of Monterey Bay was the first close European observation of the Santa Cruz shoreline.

By the eighteenth century, Spain's empire had seemed to be waning; but in 1759 Charles III became king and sought to halt the military decline of Spain. The expansion of the mission system in the New World was part of his plan, for the Spanish missions would transform Indians into colonists and supply the necessary manpower for settlement of this remote, northern frontier.

In 1768 Don Gaspar de Portolá, governor of Baja California, was sent to locate Monterey Bay. Portolá was accompanied by Father Junípero Serra, in charge of spiritual matters of the missions of Baja. The military, under Portolá, took care of the everyday management of the mission system.

The plight of the Portolá expedition was desperate by the time it reached San Diego in 1769. But Portolá continued north to find

Above: The Pajaro River forms Santa Cruz County's southern boundary with Monterey County. The river was named "Rio del Pajaro" or "river of the bird" by members of the Portolá expedition in 1769 when they found a large, stuffed bird the native Costanoans had left near the river. One of the expedition's diarists described the riverbank as "verdant and pleasant," much as it appears today. Courtesy, Jennie and Denzil Verardo

Left: In the eighteenth century, the Spaniard Don Gaspar de Portolá commanded the first European overland exploration across what is today Santa Cruz County. Noted artist Joseph Jacinto Mora drew this sketch in 1949 representing that expedition. Portolá is in the center flanked by Sergeant Ortega (left) and Padre Crespi. Courtesy, Jo Mora Publications

A PUEBLO AND A PIRATE

the ultimate objective of this exploration, Monterey Bay, while Serra remained in San Diego, where he founded California's first mission.

When Portolá and his men reached Monterey, they did not recognize the bay since they could see nothing of the exemplary harbor described 167 years earlier. The expedition pressed northward, continuing to search for Vizcaíno's ideal port.

On Sunday, October 8, 1769, the party pitched camp on the bank of the Pajaro River. In his diary, cartographer Miguel Costanso described a Costanoan Indian village near their camp, which had been burned and deserted. Left behind was a large stuffed bird which Costanso relates was the reason they named the river "Rio del Pajaro," or "River of the Bird."

Crossing the Pajaro River, the expedition came upon something that no European had seen up to this point—California's magnificent redwood trees. Because of the trees' dark, reddish color, the Spaniards named them *palo colorado,* which became "redwood" in English.

Continuing northward, the party crossed Soquel Creek and "El Rio de San Lorenzo." The San Lorenzo was named by Portolá after St. Lawrence on whose day the river was crossed.

Pressing ever northward, Portolá's party was fatigued by lack of sleep and wet from rains. On October 22, the party rested on a beach at the mouth of a valley. While there, a chronicler wrote "God had sent them health . . . , and in a short time [they] were entirely recovered . . ." For this reason the valley was named "La Salud," meaning "health." Cañada de la Salud is the present-day Waddell Creek area.

By January 1770 the entire party was back in San Diego, having failed to find Monterey Bay. Later that year, on another journey up the coast, Portolá realized Vizcaíno's exaggeration and "found" the bay. On June 3, 1770, a presidio of earth and poles was completed at Monterey.

Spain's goals in the New World were met by the establishment not only of presidios (military strongholds), but also of pueblos (civilian settlements) and missions (religious centers).

In 1774 Father Francisco Palou accompanied an expedition to San Francisco Bay. Father Palou recommended the banks of the San Lorenzo as a site for a pueblo (town) and a mission. In 1791 Father Lasuen, who led the missionary system following Serra's death, explored the site of Palou's proposed mission and raised a cross where Mission Santa Cruz, or "Holy Cross," was to be constructed. On September 25, 1791, Mission Santa Cruz was completed and Don Hermenegildo Sal, commander of San Francisco, took official possession of it. Sal then returned to San Francisco, leaving Luis Peralta in charge of the new mission.

By December, 89 Indians were at the mission, and beans and wheat had been planted. The cornerstone for the church was laid

Below: Miguel Costanso, a lieutenant with Portolá's expedition, drew this map of California's coastal geography in the early 1770s, soon after they completed their journey. In Santa Cruz County, the San Lorenzo and Pajaro rivers still bear the names given them by Portolá's party as seen on Costanso's map. Courtesy, Bibliotheque Nationale, Paris

in 1793 and the building itself was dedicated in 1794. A construction program was begun that by 1796 produced a house, workshops, corrals, a granary, and a flour mill.

Mission Santa Cruz increased its herd from 130 cattle in 1791 to 8,000 head in 1834. The development of large cattle herds was considered an economic necessity, for it was cattle which provided tallow for candle and soap making, hides for leather products, and meat for the local population.

Hides and tallow were traded to foreign merchants in return for general merchandise. This trade flourished throughout Spanish California, and Santa Cruz was no exception. Even though the Santa Cruz shoreline and harbor were not good for landing and exchanging cargo, one merchant company, McCulloch-Hartnell, did make regular stops.

But the main purpose of the missions was to control and Christianize the native population. The Indians of Mission Santa Cruz were a subjugated population. Some had entered the mission voluntarily for the food available there and the care they received. But others were forced to go to the mission. Resistance by the Costanoans was dealt with harshly. When Father Andres Quintana was murdered by several Indians in 1812, the suspects were tried and sent to Mexico for sentencing. The Indians claimed that they had murdered Father Quintana because of his cruelty. Spanish officials, however, called Quintana a model of kindness and sentenced the accused to 200 lashes each and imprisonment in chains from two to 10 years. Only one survived the punishment.

One Costanoan, Lorenzo Asesara, left an eyewitness account of life at the Santa Cruz Mission. Born in 1819 at the mission, Asesara remembered that it was the Indian children that were brought to Mission Santa Cruz. The parents would soon follow and bring their relatives. All would then be Christianized through baptism. Asesara pointed out that "the Indians were severely treated by the padres ... We were always trembling with fear of the lash." The Indians cultivated the land and tended crops. Surplus products were sold to vessels that came to Santa Cruz. Russians "carried away the wheat and barley, Spanish vessels [took] beans, corn, dried peas, and dried horse beans. English vessels carried away hides and tallow."

The Indian population at Mission Santa Cruz reached its peak in 1796 with 523 neophytes. After 1796 the native population at the mission declined due to several factors including the Indians' lack of immunity to smallpox and measles, the spread of syphilis, and inadequate nutrition. By 1830 there were 86 percent more deaths at the mission than baptisms, with measles taking the greatest toll on the Indians. During the 1827-1828 measles epidemic which spread throughout Alta California, 417 Indians died at Santa Cruz. By 1850 California's first United States Indian agent, Adam Johnston, stated that scarcely an individual Costanoan was left.

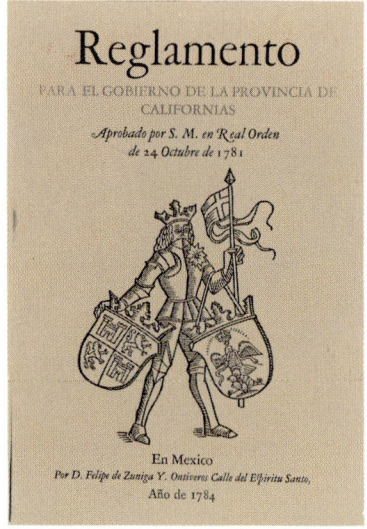

Above: In 1779, at the Royal Presidio of Monterey, the Spanish governor of California, Don Felipe de Neve, drafted a set of regulations for governing the "Province of the Californias." Courtesy, Grabhorn Press

Below: Justiniano Roxas was a Costanoan, or a member of one of the neighboring native cultures. He survived through the Spanish, Mexican, and into the American period in Santa Cruz. Courtesy, University of California, Santa Cruz, Special Collections

A PUEBLO AND A PIRATE

Above: Santa Cruz was the site of one of California's 21 Spanish missions. The painting shown here was by the Frenchman, Le Trousset, who visited Santa Cruz in 1853, and is the only known work showing the mission in its original state.

Left: Marriages were meticulously recorded at California's missions, and Santa Cruz was no exception, as this title page from Mission Santa Cruz's record of marriages illustrates. From H.A. Van Coenen Torchiana, *Story of the Mission Santa Cruz*, 1933

15

SANTA CRUZ COUNTY

In 1796 the Marques de Branciforte, viceroy of Mexico, made plans for a town to be settled by retired soldiers and their families. This new pueblo would join the two which had already been settled in California by civilians. These new settlers could act as a militia should a foreign threat occur, and at the same time create a self-supporting settlement. A location near Mission Santa Cruz was finally selected as the site of the new pueblo. On January 25, 1797, Governor Diégo de Borica proceeded with the establishment of the pueblo.

The Villa de Branciforte, as the new town was called, never met its founders' expectations. Governor Borica had trouble finding honorable, industrious, loyal volunteers to relocate to Branciforte. As a result, vagrants and criminals were shipped to the new settlement. In 1803 Commandante José Guerra Noriega wrote to the governor that the settlers of Branciforte were "not so bad as other convicts sent to California; still . . . , their absence for a couple of centuries at a distance of a million leagues would prove most beneficial to the province . . ."

Other difficulties occurred that would become major obstacles to the success of Villa de Branciforte. Adequate financing of the new pueblo never was provided and the town was constructed poorly. Areas most suitable for cultivation belonged to the mission which also held a virtual monopoly on trade with the presidios. Any surplus agricultural products that could have been produced by the pueblo would have lacked markets.

Above: Large ranchos were granted throughout Santa Cruz County when California was under the rule of Mexico. This drawing illustrates the adeptness to which the Californios handled both horses and lassos. From *Narrative of a Voyage to the Pacific,* 1831

Below: Branciforte, precursor of the city of Santa Cruz, was one of California's three official Spanish pueblos. The town was well planned, as shown in this 1796 proposal for the pueblo's development. Unfortunately, actual construction was poor due to a lack of engineers at Branciforte, and most of the buildings resembled little more than shacks. Courtesy, Jennie and Denzil Verardo

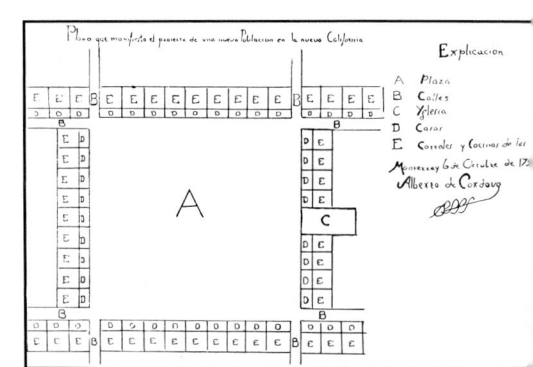

A PUEBLO AND A PIRATE

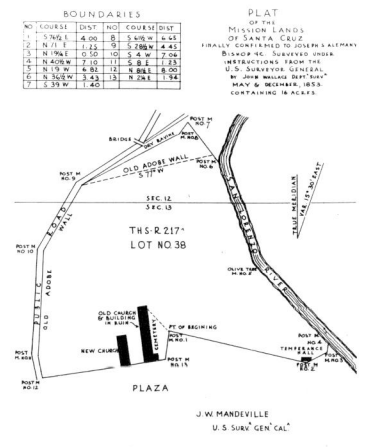

Above: In the 1850s, after California had become a part of the United States, mission lands were surveyed to determine what would remain in the possession of the Catholic Church. Shown here is the original 1853 survey of Mission Santa Cruz. Courtesy, Jennie and Denzil Verardo

Below: Adobe bricks were the typical construction material associated with Spanish and Mexican California. Unfortunately few of the Santa Cruz County adobe dwellings have survived to the present. The adobe shown here in 1859 was built on Rancho Bolsa de San Cayetano (Pajaro Valley) and was located on present-day San Juan Road. It collapsed in the 1906 Earthquake. Photo by Ida Reed. Courtesy, Pajaro Valley Historical Association

The Villa de Branciforte had a population slightly over 100 in 1803, after which it began to decline. Mission Santa Cruz was declining as well. Spain, at war with England and France, could not afford to give much attention to its colonies.

In 1818 the privateer Hippolyte de Bouchard landed in Monterey, and looted and plundered the town. Flying the flag of Buenos Aires (Argentina), Bouchard claimed to be operating for the cause of the revolution against Spain, to which California was still technically loyal.

When news of Bouchard's attack reached Santa Cruz, the mission was abandoned. Governor Pablo Vicente de Solá ordered the leader of Branciforte, Commisionado Joaquin Buelna, to remove any remaining mission property. Later some would contend that the citizenry of Branciforte looted the mission, and destruction of property did indeed occur. Many Costanoans took this opportunity to flee the confines of the mission.

After burning Monterey and causing hysteria across the bay, Bouchard sailed south without ever landing in the Santa Cruz area.

Revolt against Spanish rule in Mexico resulted in that country's independence in 1821. The new Mexican government made generous grants of land to loyal citizens in Alta California.

Prior to the revolution, land grants had been made by the Spanish government including Rancho Salsipuedes in the Pajaro Valley. The northeast section of the rancho provided grazing land for sheep from Mission Santa Cruz. Following the Mexican Revolution, Salsipuedes became a 31,201-acre land grant ceded in 1840 to Manuel Jimeño, secretary of state to Governors Alvarado and Micheltorena between 1839 and 1845.

In 1834 Mexico secularized California's missions. The churches themselves were generally the only portion left under religious control. The Indians at Mission Santa Cruz were given Spanish surnames and much of the mission's goods were distributed among them. Mission Santa Cruz effectively ceased to exist.

Secularization freed former Church lands for civilian settlement. Besides Salsipuedes, more than a dozen ranchos were granted in present-day Santa Cruz County.

Meanwhile, American interest in the West and particularly in California was growing, encouraged by the reports of fur traders and merchants, and inspired by the doctrine of Manifest Destiny. Conflicts between the new American settlers and the Californios were bound to occur, and Santa Cruz County settlers played no small part in these conflicts.

Isaac Graham, a trapper, rifleman, and mountain man, worked his way west to California and became a central figure in its history. Graham settled in Santa Cruz County and made his living producing and selling whiskey. In 1836, when Juan Bautista Alvarado began a revolt against the Mexican governor, he enlisted the aid of Graham,

17

Above: General John Charles Fremont's exploring party had a reunion in 1888, shown here, at the Big Trees Hotel near Felton. Fremont's party played an important part in the Mexican War and the ultimate surrender of Mexican forces to the U.S. in California. Courtesy, Covello & Covello Photographers

who recruited a band of riflemen from the Santa Cruz area. Alvarado succeeded in his coup and became governor.

Governor Alvarado, seeing Graham and his friends as ungovernable and believing that an uprising by American settlers was imminent, ordered the arrest of all foreigners between Monterey and San Francisco. Some of these immigrants were later freed, but Isaac Graham and about a dozen of his associates from the Santa Cruz area were shipped to Mexico, accused of plotting against the government.

Through intervention by the British Consul, Graham was acquitted and released. He and his followers were given free passage back to California and a cash settlement. Graham settled on Rancho Zayante in the Santa Cruz Mountains, and soon built the county's first sawmill.

In 1842 Manuel Micheltorena became governor of California. In 1844 a revolt was begun under Alvarado's leadership. Graham joined Micheltorena's forces against Alvarado, while other foreigners joined Alvarado. In 1845 the armies met at Cahuenga Pass in Southern California. Perceiving that they had nothing to gain in this battle, the foreign contingents on both sides pulled out, ending further fighting. Micheltorena eventually withdrew from California. Alvarado recognized Pio Pico as the new governor and José Castro as California's military commander.

Graham returned to his rancho. In 1851 he purchased Rancho Punta del Año Nuevo on the north coast of the new county and had a house constructed there. Later, because of Graham's heavy debts,

A PUEBLO AND A PIRATE

Above: This hollowed redwood, located in present-day Henry Cowell Redwoods State Park, purportedly sheltered John Charles Fremont. The famous pathfinder camped in the Santa Cruz Mountains during one of his treks in the West. Courtesy, Jennie and Denzil Verardo

Right: Clearing a patch in the forest to build a home was a task faced by many of the county's early settlers. Emigrants from the United States, arriving in Mexican California through the 1840s, often became citizens of Mexico, a requirement for obtaining a grant of land in Mexican territories. However, with the influx of Americans, Mexico's hold on California began to weaken. This turn-of-the-century photo is by Andrew P. Hill. Courtesy, Sempervirens Fund

the rancho was sold at public auction.

Historian Hubert Howe Bancroft described Graham as "... a loud-mouthed, unprincipled, profligate, and a reckless man, whose only good qualities seem to have been the personal bravery and prodigal hospitality of his class, with undoubted skill as a hunter, and a degree of industry." Isaac Graham died in 1863 at the age of 70 and is buried in the Evergreen Cemetery in Santa Cruz.

Other "foreign" settlers in Santa Cruz County began early businesses. In 1843 Paul Sweet established the first tannery in what would become Scotts Valley. Joseph Majors, who had been arrested with Graham, opened and operated the area's first gristmill. Their arrival, along with many others, signalled the beginning of the end of Mexican rule in California.

The United States government had become increasingly interested in California during the 1840s, and sent John C. Fremont on several western expeditions. In February 1846, during one of these "scientific" explorations, Fremont camped in the Santa Cruz Mountains in what is now Henry Cowell Redwoods State Park. The party then moved north, and while staying near Sacramento, a large number of American settlers gathered at his camp for protection. Alarmed by rumors that the Mexican government was about to forbid further immigration into California, they were fearful of a confrontation.

A group of men left Fremont's camp in June 1846 bound for Sonoma, headquarters and home of the influential Mexican general, Mariano Vallejo. In Sonoma the band bloodlessly hauled down the Mexican flag and declared California a republic. The republic's existence was short-lived, however, as war soon broke out between the United States and Mexico.

Fremont enlisted American volunteers and formed the California Battalion of Mounted Riflemen. Many of the Americans in Santa Cruz joined Fremont on his march against Mexico, which ended when Fremont received a capitulation from Andrés Pico at Cahuenga in Southern California. With the treaty of Guadalupe-Hidalgo in 1848, the war ended and Alta California became a territory of the United States.

SANTA CRUZ COUNTY

Utilizing the San Lorenzo Flume, companies could float their lumber down to Felton to be loaded on to railroad cars for shipment to the Santa Cruz Wharf. In the 1860s and 1870s, the flume was the most efficient means of transporting lumber down the valley. Courtesy, UCSC Special Collections

Chapter Two

REDWOODS TO ROLLER COASTERS

The raising of the American flag over Santa Cruz County heralded changes which would indelibly mark the face of the area. When American settlers arrived with their energy, enthusiasm, and audacity, they put an abrupt end to the placidity of the rancho period. There were industries to be started, natural resources to be tapped, and fortunes to be made.

Even the decades-old dispute over the prominence of Branciforte or Santa Cruz was quickly settled by the Americans. Branciforte was one of the original 27 counties of the new state of California. The county's name was changed to Santa Cruz by the state legislature in 1850, and the name was never questioned after that.

Several industries which were started by American immigrants before the Bear Flag Revolt provided the starting point for economic development in the new county. Building on the foundation laid by Paul Sweet in 1843, the tanning industry grew and prospered. By 1870 there were nine tanneries in operation in the county with an annual income of $382,800.

Chief among these was the Kron Tanning Company located on River Street near the town of Santa Cruz. The tannery was built in 1855, rebuilt after the floods of 1861-1862, and purchased by

Jacob Kron in 1866. The capacity of the steam-powered plant was 250 sides of sole leather per day. The plant is still in operation as the A.K. Salz Tannery, having been sold by the Kron family to Kullman and Salz in 1918.

As important as the tanning industry was in Santa Cruz County, its decline began soon after its initial success. Tan oak bark, one of the county's natural resources, became scarce, since stripping the bark killed the trees. By 1881 bark was being imported for up to $16 per cord. Without an abundant, cheap source of tan oak bark, many of the tanneries could not afford to stay in operation.

In earlier, less mechanized times, communities developed local industries to satisfy their needs. Flour production in Santa Cruz County had its origins in the mission period. The mission mill was erected in the late 1790s. After secularization of the missions, a Russian, José Antonio Bolcoff, took possession of the mill. In 1866 the mill became the property of John Prewett and Joseph Riley.

Joseph Majors, who had come to the Santa Cruz area in 1835, established several gristmills, the first of which was in Scotts Valley. In 1839 Majors married Maria de los Angeles Castro, and soon acquired two land grants, San Augustin (Scotts Valley) and Zayante, in addition to managing his wife's 12,000-acre Rancho Refugio on the coast. Majors built a waterpowered gristmill on Escalona Heights where he built a large home for Maria and their 19 children. Majors was a prominent local citizen, serving as alcalde for Santa

Above, left: Limestone, shown here being transported from a Cowell quarry by an ox team, proved to be one of the more valuable resources of the county. By 1860 all but about $10,000 worth of the state's total output was produced in Santa Cruz kilns. Courtesy, UCSC Special Collections

Above, right: The Henry Cowell Lime Company kilns were located about three and a half miles north of Santa Cruz at the Rincon. The processed lime was taken down to Santa Cruz where it was loaded on schooners for transport up and down the coast. Courtesy, UCSC Special Collections

Right: Mr. and Mrs. Henry Cowell, shown here circa 1900, had a ranch in Santa Cruz which the family abandoned after the accidental death of daughter Sarah in 1903. Although there were five Cowell children, there were no grandchildren. The family dynasty ended in February 1955, with the death of Samuel H. Cowell at age 93. Courtesy, UCSC Special Collections

REDWOODS TO ROLLER COASTERS

Cruz during the Mexican period and as the first treasurer of the new Santa Cruz County.

In 1860 six mills produced over $100,000 worth of flour in Santa Cruz County. The census of 1880 showed no gristmills left in the county. As in the rest of California, small mills were replaced by mass-production factories.

Isaac E. Davis and Albion P. Jordan were two more American entrepreneurs who would help fashion the new county. Arriving in California with the Forty-Niners, Davis and Jordan decided that their fortunes lay with limestone rather than with gold. Lime was to become an essential element in construction in the new state. It was needed for mortar and cement.

In 1851 they constructed the first limekiln in Santa Cruz County, which may have been the first in the state. By 1880 over 114,500 barrels of lime, valued at $325,000, were annually made in the county.

Davis and Jordan had a steamship, the *Santa Cruz,* built in 1856, and eventually they built up a small fleet of schooners. They also bought the county's first wharf from its builder, Elihu Anthony, and had it widened to accommodate tramcars carrying lime.

Due to failing health, Jordan sold his interest in the company to Henry Cowell in 1864. By 1866 the Davis and Cowell Lime and Cement Company was the largest of the three such enterprises in the county, providing 60,000 of the 140,000 barrels of lime produced. In 1878 Santa Cruz County generated $200,000 worth of lime and produced one-half of the demands of the state. Upon Davis' death in 1880, the company became the Henry Cowell Lime Company.

The Cowell family was not only one of the wealthiest in California, but also one of the most philanthropic. Much of the family's wealth eventually went to charities and public institutions. Of special significance to Santa Cruz County were two such contributions—Henry Cowell Redwoods State Park, a memorial that Samuel H. Cowell created for his father; and the site of the Cowell ranch, upon which stands the University of California at Santa Cruz.

The IXL Company and the Holmes Lime Kiln Company also had quarries and kilns operating in the county. Santa Cruz lime was considered superior to any in the state.

Paper production was another early industry which required lime. A young San Francisco gold bullion broker, Henry Van Valkenburgh, recognized that Santa Cruz County possessed the resources needed to make paper manufacture profitable. In addition to the abundant lime resources, the area also had sufficient waterpower for a mill along the San Lorenzo River, and the great wheat fields of the Pajaro Valley could supply the straw. Van Valkenburgh purchased a portion of Sainsevain's Rancho Cañada del Rincon and built the first paper mill in October 1860. The San Francisco *Daily Alta California* commented in August 1860 that

SANTA CRUZ COUNTY

... besides a monopoly of lime and leather, Santa Cruz is about to have a monopoly of straw paper ... It [the mill] will produce fifty tons of straw paper a month. The amount of such paper now imported to California exceeds fifty tons per month and it costs, delivered in the wharf in San Francisco, about $100 per ton to the importer. So this mill will save the state $60,000 a year.

A 3,460-foot flume assured a water supply to the mill from the dam which was built upstream on the river. In February 1861, during a heavy storm, the San Lorenzo River flooded, taking out the paper mill dam. Van Valkenburgh had the damage quickly repaired and the San Lorenzo Paper Mill was soon back in operation.

During the winter of 1861-1862 major portions of California were flooded as intense storms turned even placid rivers like the San Lorenzo into raging torrents. Again the river ravaged the mill; in an even greater tragedy, Henry Van Valkenburgh lost his life to a falling tree. Eventually the mill became part of the California Powder Works property.

Henry Van Valkenburgh was not the only early industrialist to recognize the county's advantageous resources for papermaking. Edward and Frank O'Neill and Peter and James Brown also established mills in the county. But as farming in Santa Cruz County changed, the abundant supply of straw was lost to the mills and eventually all shut down.

An industry which was established to meet the needs of both the new state and of the developing nation was destined to become the county's chief industrial feature for half a century.

Blasting powder had become a precious commodity in California by the late 1850s. Besides the demand for powder for mining, the construction of the transcontinental railroad would require large amounts of explosives. With the imminent threat of civil war, the U.S. government banned shipping of powder by sea to prevent its seizure by the Confederacy. It was in this setting that the California Powder Works was begun.

The men with the foresight to envision powder mill operations on the San Lorenzo incorporated as the California Powder Works in December 1861, with John H. Baird as president. The California Powder Works went into operation in May 1864, and by 1896 the historical narrative *Beautiful Santa Cruz* boasted that CPW was "rated as second to none in Europe or America, whether the magnitude of their operations be considered, or their skillful use of the best knowledge of their art ..."

The powder works, for years the largest employer in Santa Cruz County, had from 80 to 275 employees at various times. Included at the works were 21 powder mills, 10 shops, six magazines and stores, and 34 other buildings. By 1887 four million pounds of powder was the annual yield.

Above: Bitumin mines, like the City Street Improvement Company's 1914 operation shown here, declined with the advent of cement as a paving material. Courtesy, UCSC Special Collections

REDWOODS TO ROLLER COASTERS

The California Powder Works was the first company on the Pacific Coast to produce nitro-cotton smokeless powder for cannon. It became one of two suppliers of the powder to the U.S. government during the Spanish-American War. CPW also produced brown prismatic powder for high-power breech-loading cannon. This powder was so highly regarded that CPW supplied all of the powder for the Pacific and Asiatic fleets of the U.S. and for Pacific harbor and shore defenses in the late 1800s. Much of the credit for these innovations must go to Bernard Peyton, superintendent of CPW beginning in 1898, and to his son, William C. Peyton.

In 1867 Alfred Nobel developed dynamite and radically changed the explosives industry. CPW continued to manufacture powder and never did produce dynamite. The DuPont Company began acquiring CPW before 1900, and in 1906 the California Powder Works officially became part of the DuPont empire. Powder production was moved from the Santa Cruz site in 1914, and in 1924 the powder works area was sold to the Masonic Lodge to become Paradise Park.

An early leader in the county's industrial development was Elihu Anthony. Many firsts belong to Anthony. He built the first foundry in the area in 1848, where he cast the first iron plows in California and produced the first picks for the gold mines. He built the first commercial building below Mission Hill, starting a movement which resulted in the location of the current commercial center of the city. Anthony built the first wharf in Santa Cruz in 1849, laid

w: This 1880s photo shows the ll Wharf (rear), which had built by Elihu Anthony, and ailroad Wharf, terminus for outh Pacific Coast Railroad. tesy, UCSC Special Collections

out the first real estate subdivisions, was instrumental in the establishment of the first Protestant church in the area, and served as the first postmaster of Santa Cruz. In addition, he was the first president of the first county Board of Supervisors.

The energy, enthusiasm, and business acumen with which Elihu Anthony approached life was matched by another settler in Santa Cruz, Frederick A. Hihn. Born in Germany in 1829, he set sail for California in 1849. In 1851 Hihn opened a mercantile store in Santa Cruz. Through hard work and determination, Hihn amassed a personal fortune. But it had taken its toll on his health, and Hihn turned his mercantile business over to his brother Hugo in 1857.

Now he could turn his attention to his real estate holdings. Hihn's operations extended to all parts of the county, and ultimately his company owned 15,000 acres. At one point, Hihn owned one-sixth of the land in the county and held mortgages on much of the rest. His method was to purchase large tracts of land, develop roads and landscaping, and generally improve the area. He subdivided these tracts into lots and parcels and sold them on terms which were agreeable to the buyer.

A man with many firsts to his credit, Hihn not only founded Capitola, but built the wharf that is there now. He changed the name from La Playa de Soquel when he built his resort, Camp Capitola, there in 1869. Hihn and Anthony were involved with the Santa Clara Turnpike Company which in 1858 built the first wagon road over the Santa Cruz Mountains into the Santa Clara Valley. Hihn also built the first horsecar line in the county, the *Red Line,* which ran from the Lower Plaza (Pacific Avenue and Front Street) to Leibbrandt's Bathhouse on the waterfront.

Not content to stop with a streetcar line, Hihn joined forces with Claus Spreckels to construct a railroad line from Watsonville to Santa Cruz. The Santa Cruz Railroad was formed in June 1873, and Hihn served as the company president until 1881.

Hihn, along with Elihu Anthony, organized the county's first water system in 1860. He also was instrumental in organizing the City Bank and the City Savings Bank of Santa Cruz, and managed to serve as a school trustee, a county supervisor, and as a member of the state assembly.

But Hihn's lumbering concerns may have produced his greatest impact on the county. There were cutting operations and mills at Valencia in the Santa Cruz Mountains as well as a planing mill in Monterey County. The Valencia Mill alone had a daily capacity of 70,000 board feet of lumber!

Frederick Hihn was not the only entrepreneur to recognize the wealth that lay in Santa Cruz County's lush redwood forests. In 1857 there were 10 sawmills in the county with a total capacity of 40,000 feet of lumber per day. By 1864 there were 28 sawmills in the San Lorenzo Valley alone, cutting 34 million feet of lumber per year.

Above: Ox teams were used to drag logs down skid roads to the lumber mill. Companies such as the Loma Prieta Lumber Company shown here circa 1890 were forced to leave excessively large trees standing for lack of an efficient method of felling them. So most logs were of a fairly standard size. Courtesy, UCSC Special Collections

Right: Frederick A. Hihn, shown in a 1903 portrait, was not only a civic leader, businessman, and real estate developer, but he also founded Capitola and started the first streetcar line in the county. Courtesy, Jennie and Denzil Verardo

Below, right: The geographical features of Santa Cruz County are detailed in this 1879 map which also shows railroad and steamboat routes of the day. From Wallace W. Elliott & Co., *Santa Cruz County, California,* 1879

REDWOODS TO ROLLER COASTERS

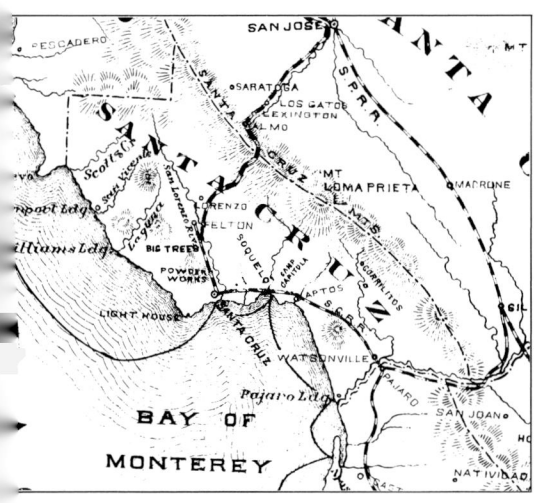

In 1847, to facilitate transportation of the lumber, the California legislature passed an act providing for construction of a 20-mile-long flume from the headwaters of the San Lorenzo River near Saratoga Summit to the Pacific Ocean. There at Santa Cruz, the lumber could be shipped up and down the coast. That same year, directors of the Santa Cruz and Felton Railroad formed the San Lorenzo Flume and Lumber Company. Their plan was to build the flume down to Felton, but to substitute their rail service on to the waterfront. The company constructed a tunnel under Mission Hill and laid tracks down Chestnut Street paralleling the tracks of Hihn's Santa Cruz Railroad. The narrow-gauge Santa Cruz and Felton Railroad commenced service in 1876, with a line that ran from Felton to the waterfront terminating at the rechristened Railroad Wharf.

In July 1879 the South Pacific Coast Railroad leased the tracks, rolling stock, and flume of the Santa Cruz and Felton line. Direct service was then extended from Santa Cruz to San Jose, Oakland, and the East Bay.

In 1882 Southern Pacific acquired Hihn's Santa Cruz Railroad through bankruptcy proceedings, taking charge of the company's standard-gauge line in 1883. Connections were then assured with the main Southern Pacific line which ran through Pajaro.

As Santa Cruz County became more accessible, development intensified, causing an increase in the demand for redwood lumber. However, in the late 1800s the beginnings of a preservation movement were stirring. There were some who feared that if the frantic pace of logging continued, the redwoods would be gone forever.

In the fall of 1899 Andrew P. Hill was commissioned by a magazine to take photographs of the redwoods in the Santa Cruz Mountains. Hill selected the Felton Grove, which at that time was in private ownership and was run as a tourist attraction. He was told by the owner that "no photographs [of the trees] were allowed to be taken by an outsider, as they were the prerequisites of the hotel." Hill would later comment, "I was a little angry and somewhat disgusted with my reception at the Santa Cruz big trees . . . the thought flashed through my mind that these trees because of their size and antiquity, were among the natural wonders of the world, and should be saved for posterity. I said to myself, 'I will start a campaign immediately to make a public park of this place.'"

Hill elicited the help of Josephine Clifford McCrackin, one of the few women journalists of the day. When Hill approached McCrackin with his idea, she immediately wrote an article which appeared in the Santa Cruz *Sentinel*. "Hers was the first voice . . . to raise the rallying cry, 'Save the Redwoods,' which was our slogan," Judge John Richards of San Jose would later tell. Richards—himself a "writer of reputation,"—also wrote an article, which the Associated Press picked up, urging preservation of these trees. News of the movement thus spread across the country.

SANTA CRUZ COUNTY

Far left: The Big Trees Grove near Felton was another Santa Cruz Mountains redwood area. Lucy and Bessie Ball, whose family leased the resort, are shown here near the railroad platform. Courtesy, California Department of Parks and Recreation

Above, left: The Sempervirens Club poses at an early meeting in Big Basin. Andrew Hill, the founder of the movement, is the white-haired, white-bearded man in the dark suit seated in a chair in the center-front of the photo. Courtesy, Sempervirens Fund

Left: On May 1, 1900, at Stanford University, the first meeting of the group which would preserve Big Basin was held. Andrew Hill organized the meeting, but was also the official photographer, so he is not seen in the photo. Courtesy, Sempervirens Fund

Above: Josephine Clifford McCrackin, seated, was one of the most famous early Santa Cruz writers. Also an ardent conservationist, she coined the slogan "Save the Redwoods" for the Sempervirens Club's campaign to preserve Big Basin. Courtesy, UCSC Special Collections

The Santa Cruz Board of Trade asked Congress for an appropriation to establish a redwood park. At the urging of J.F. Coope of the Santa Cruz Board of Trade, Andrew Hill called a public meeting to solidify support for a public park. The meeting was held at Stanford University on May 1, 1900. The group, composed of many of the most influential citizens of the day, turned its attention to Big Basin, north of Boulder Creek. Two members of the group, Stanford Professors William Dudley and Colonel Wing, had explored the basin and mapped it when the university was considering purchase of that tract. Their enthusiastic support led to the formation of a party to visit the area and report on it.

Hill organized a committee which started for Big Basin on May 15, 1900. It was composed of W.W. Richards, R.S. Kooser, Andrew Hill, Carrie Stevens Walter, and Mrs. S.A. Jones, all of the San Jose area; J.F. Coope and J.Q. Packard of Santa Cruz; and H.L. Middleton, representing the lumber company which held options on most of the Big Basin lands. They were joined later by Charles Wesley Reed of the San Francisco Board of Supervisors. After several days of exploring, the group was convinced that Big Basin should be preserved as a public park. On May 18, 1900, the Sempervirens Club was organized. Charles W. Reed was elected president and the fight to save the redwoods was on!

Andrew Hill and the Sempervirens Club worked long, diligent hours to convince both the public and the legislature that Big Basin had to be preserved as a public park. H.L. Middleton, though a lumberman, saw the value in preservation, and helped the Sempervirens Club secure a one-year option on Big Basin to delay cutting of the trees. Reed drafted legislation to create a California Redwood Park Commission and to appropriate $500,000 for purchase of redwood forest land. The bill was introduced by San Francisco Assemblyman George H. Fisk, and Hill traveled to Sacramento to convince not only the legislature, but also a reluctant governor to support the bill with the appropriation cut in half. On March 16, 1901, Governor Henry T. Gage signed the legislation which gave California its first state park.

The actual purchase was completed in September 1902. The California Redwood Park in Big Basin consisted of 3,800 acres. Twenty-five hundred acres of prime virgin redwoods were purchased, and H.L. Middleton, now a member of the Sempervirens Club, arranged the donation of an additional 1,300 acres of neighboring cut-over and brush lands. The establishment of the state park added greatly to the area's attractiveness to tourists.

But when Santa Cruz County's tourist industry is considered, there can be no doubt as to its dominant promoter—Fred Willer Swanton. In fact, his impact was so great that the city was once labeled "Swanta Cruz."

Fred Swanton came to Santa Cruz from New York in 1866 at

SANTA CRUZ COUNTY

Left: Water wagons such as this one kept dust down on the wagon road into the new state park. Immediate use of the park was delayed by a major fire in September 1904, which burned everything except the area around Governor's Camp at the park's center. Courtesy, Sempervirens Fund

Below, left: In 1901 legislation created a Redwood Park Commission to purchase parkland. In September 1901 commissioners visited Big Basin on an inspection tour. Governor Henry T. Gage is at center with the bow tie. Father Robert Kenna, with collar, was an instrumental member of both the Sempervirens Club and the commission. Courtesy, Jennie and Denzil Verardo

Right: After the acquisition of Big Basin, the Sempervirens Club continued its involvement in the area. In 1919 the club presented the first annual forest play, *The Soul of Sequoia.* Nymphs from the production, which took place in Big Basin, are pictured here. Courtesy, Sempervirens Fund

the age of four. Two years after graduating from Heald's Business College in San Francisco in 1881, Swanton and his father entered the tourism business by constructing a grand, three-story hotel on Front Street in Santa Cruz. After the hotel was destroyed by fire, the younger Swanton started the Santa Cruz Light and Power Company in 1889, with Dr. H.H. Clark as his partner. Two years later, he organized the Santa Cruz, Garfield Park and Capitola Electric Railway Company. Businessman James P. Smith was Swanton's partner in the enterprise which gave the county its first electric streetcar system.

In 1896 Swanton began one of his most ambitious projects by founding the Big Creek Power Company. Pushing through 18 miles of power line from the plant in Big Creek Canyon to Santa Cruz, Swanton supplied power to his railway and electric light company as well as eventually to most of the county.

By 1903 Swanton was preparing to begin work on his dream of creating a West Coast Coney Island amusement park in Santa Cruz. As early as the 1850s, vacationers had come to the area to enjoy the Pacific Ocean House, the St. Charles Hotel, and the Pope House in the city of Santa Cruz, and the nearby resort of Camp Capitola. In 1887 C.F. Miller's Neptune Baths joined the original Leibbrandt's Bathhouses as oceanside attractions. These pleasure spots became the primary destinations of the early streetcar lines, assuring their use by locals as well as by tourists.

In 1903 Fred Swanton organized the Santa Cruz Beach Cottage

and Tent City Corporation. With the backing of investors which included Southern Pacific Railroad, Swanton purchased the Miller and Leibbrandt bathhouses and began work on his casino, pleasure pier, and tent city resort. The Moorish-style casino opened in 1904 and was an unquestioned success. Swanton personally made a series of promotional tours on its behalf throughout California, after convincing Southern Pacific to provide a special train for the tours. His efforts are credited with bringing some 100,000 additional visitors to Santa Cruz.

On June 22, 1906, while Swanton was on one of his trips, the casino burned to the ground. All that was left of the uninsured $204,000 investment were portions of the tent city, a part of the pleasure pier, and the hot baths. Undaunted, Fred Swanton reformed the company into the Santa Cruz Beach Company, raised $750,000 in capital, and built a larger casino, an extended boardwalk, and an indoor swimming pool. The new facility opened on June 15, 1907, a week less than one year after the fire. In the meantime, Swanton had managed to not only immediately reopen the baths, but to host the State Republican Convention in September 1906 under a large canvas tent at the beach.

Above: **This photo shows the Santa Cruz Beach boardwalk in 1910. Courtesy, UCSC Special Collections**

Above, far right: **Fred Swanton's dream resort and playland opened in 1904 and featured this Moorish-style casino. Two years later, it burned to the ground. The reorganized Santa Cruz Beach Company quickly replaced it with a new building. Courtesy, Jennie and Denzil Verardo**

REDWOODS TO ROLLER COASTERS

Top: Beautiful ocean scenery induced tourists to visit the county. These turn-of-the-century beachcombers seem to be enjoying the beach even though they appear dressed for the city. Courtesy, UCSC Special Collections

Bottom: Not all of Santa Cruz County's tourists stayed at hotels and resorts. Some, like W.W. Richards, preferred the simple pleasures of camp life. Courtesy, Sempervirens Fund

Swanton and his family organized the Swanton Investment Company in 1908 to develop a subdivision on West Cliff Drive. In 1910 Swanton undertook construction of the Casa del Rey Hotel across from his casino. Unfortunately for Fred Swanton, this was also when his amazing resiliency and luck seemed to run out.

The Swanton Beach Park subdivision did not prove successful, and eventually the beach property went to the state to become a park. The $500,000 cost of the Casa del Rey Hotel and an economic recession were too much for the Santa Cruz Beach Company. The casino and boardwalk were later sold to the Santa Cruz Seaside Company, which would add the landmark Giant Dipper roller coaster a few years later, but Fred Swanton was forced into bankruptcy in 1912.

Slowed down but not stopped, Swanton organized the Pan-Pacific Exposition in San Francisco in 1915. By 1916 he was on a slight rebound due to some investments in chrome mining. Fred Swanton was not a quitter. And he never gave up on Santa Cruz! He served as its mayor from 1927 until 1933, and was its chief promoter until his death in 1940. He was never able to regain financial stability, and when he was again declared bankrupt in 1930, his sole asset was his mayor's salary of $1,200 per year. Although Fred Swanton was almost penniless when he died, he left precious monuments.

Swanton's foresight and his confidence that Santa Cruz could be a major resort area helped establish an industry that remains vital today. He urged, and in some cases forced, modernization in Santa Cruz. His vision was matched by his determination. Fred Swanton was one of the restless and relentless shapers of this paradise.

33

SANTA CRUZ COUNTY

The All Souls Unitarian Church was located on Center Street in Santa Cruz. The tower in the background on the right was the high school. The church was built by the Reverend George Stone, who later became mayor. Courtesy, UCSC Special Collections

Chapter Three

"AS A CITY UPON A HILL"

The spirit and character of any community are embodied in its institutions. Whether judicial, humanitarian, educational, or those represented by the press or the pulpit, Santa Cruz County's institutions are an integral part of its social history.

Judicially, an "alcalde" system of civil government was in effect when California was conveyed to the United States. This Mexican system of government was retained by the U.S. since the occupied territory was not yet a state, and order had to be maintained.

Under the laws of the Republic of Mexico, the alcalde performed all legislative, executive, and judicial functions within a community. The alcalde enforced both civil and criminal laws and could render judgments in those matters. In territorial California, the alcalde functioned as the court of first instance and the U.S. military governor acted as the appellate court.

Several American alcaldes served the Santa Cruz region during this transition period, but William Blackburn was probably the most notorious. Blackburn, a cabinetmaker from Virginia, came to California in 1845 and settled in the Santa Cruz area. After fighting in Fremont's battalion against Mexico, Blackburn returned to Santa Cruz. He was appointed alcalde on June 21, 1847, by Acting Military Governor Richard B. Mason.

Blackburn, according to the local press, "performed the duties of the office to the entire satisfaction of all," although questions were raised concerning his use of authority. All decisions were supposed to be sent by the alcaldes to the governor for approval before sentencing was carried out. William Blackburn often disregarded this regulation. In one instance, a convicted murderer was sentenced to be "conducted back to prison ... and then taken out and shot." The sentence was carried out, and then the trial and execution were reported to the military governor.

On another occasion, an individual was convicted of shearing off a horse's mane and tail. Blackburn did not delay in sentencing the guilty party to be "taken out in front of this office and there be sheared close."

Alcaldes also had the authority to grant land. Blackburn made numerous grants, but many were later declared void since records were never transmitted to the Federal Land Commission for approval. William Blackburn resigned as alcalde in 1848 to join the Gold Rush, but returned and resumed office a short time later.

The first case to be tried by an impanelled jury in California took place on September 4, 1846, and involved one of Santa Cruz County's most infamous characters, Isaac Graham. The case of *Isaac Graham vs. Charles Roussilan* involved "Property on one side and the integrity of character on the other." The verdict acquitted Roussilan of fraudulent intent, and found a balance due Graham of $65.

When statehood was granted in 1850, counties were formed and a new judicial system put in place. The California Constitution provided that the judicial power of the state would be vested in a supreme court, in district and county courts, and in justices of the peace. Justice courts inherited the alcalde's jurisdictions, and the supreme court took over the military governor's role as the appellate court. County courts were organized with nine district courts, each exercising jurisdiction over several counties. The Third District Court

Left: The Hall of Records (corner octagonal building) and courthouse (to the right of the Hall of Records) were important in Santa Cruz County's government scene. The county courthouse shown in this photo was the original 1866-built building which burned down in 1894. The Hall of Records dates from 1882, a year before this picture was taken. The building was dedicated in 1972 as the home of the Santa Cruz County Historical Museum. Courtesy, UCSC Special Collections

Above: From the founding of the mission in 1791 to the present, the Catholic Church has had an important religious presence in Santa Cruz County. Shown in this image are the old (left) and new (right) Catholic churches on Mission Hill in the city of Santa Cruz. The old church was built in 1857 and torn down in 1898, while its replacement was constructed in 1889. Courtesy, UCSC Special Collections

included Santa Cruz, Monterey, Santa Clara, and Contra Costa counties. Although the colorful era of the alcalde had ended, the first judge from Santa Cruz County was none other than William Blackburn. In 1855 he left the bench for the state assembly. An era ended when William Blackburn died in 1867.

In 1849 an early American settler in the area, Thomas Fallon, built a wooden building which served as a courthouse for the Santa Cruz area. The county's first "modern" courthouse was constructed in 1866, on land donated by the Cooper brothers. John and William Cooper were descendants of the noted author James Fenimore Cooper, and William was the first mayor of the city of Santa Cruz. In 1894 the courthouse burned down. A tax was levied for construction of a new building which was completed in 1896. That structure was heavily damaged by the 1906 Earthquake, but was rebuilt. No longer a courthouse, the building has been restored and is being preserved as the Cooper House retail complex.

In addition to organizing the court system, the California legislature of 1850 also created the office of local constable. The constable's duty was law enforcement within the township in which he was elected. The sheriff was responsible for the remainder of the county's law enforcement.

Santa Cruz County's first sheriff was Francisco Alzina who, due to political turmoil within his home country of Spain, fled by stowing away on the USS *Constitution* when it was leaving Barcelona. He arrived in California in 1846. Ideal for the job since he was fluent in both English and Spanish, Alzina served as a respected interpreter between the two cultures during this critical transition period.

As the judicial system expanded to provide for the new order of government, religious institutions increased to meet the spiritual needs of a new, more heterogeneous society.

Until the end of the mission system and Mexican rule in California, the development of religion in Santa Cruz County cannot be separated from the political history of the period. However, the strong commitment to the separation of church and state that came with U.S. control allowed religious institutions to increase dramatically throughout the area.

The old mission church was used until 1857, when part of it collapsed during an earthquake which occurred while a mass was taking place. In 1858 a new Catholic church was dedicated in Santa Cruz. In order to meet the demands of a growing parish, a larger church was built in 1889 on "Mission Hill."

In 1854 a site was selected for a Catholic church in the Pajaro Valley, two miles northeast of Watsonville. The following year the church was completed, and in 1856 it was consecrated by Thaddeus Amat, bishop of the dioceses of Monterey and Los Angeles. By 1864 construction had begun on St. Patrick's Catholic Church which was located in Watsonville proper. The new church was dedicated in

1875. A brick church was constructed in 1903 and is still in use as St. Patrick's in Watsonville.

During this same period Bishop Amat conceived the idea of an orphanage to meet the church's social needs. The Pajaro Valley was selected as the site of this institution. In 1869 the Pajaro Valley Orphan Asylum was founded. It was placed under the tutelage of the Franciscan order of Catholics from Mission Santa Barbara. Funding for the asylum was later provided by the State of California, which allotted $100 per year to the orphanage for each child in its care. The asylum eventually became the St. Francis School of Watsonville.

Five Protestant church groups were organized in the 1850s and 1860s in Santa Cruz County. The first was a Methodist church organized by Elihu Anthony in 1848. The dynamic Reverend William Taylor of San Francisco actually dedicated the first Methodist church building, a 20-by-30-foot wooden structure, in 1850. Taylor declared that when he came to Santa Cruz he found "the largest Sunday School in the country" in operation.

In the 1850s two other Methodist congregations were organized in Watsonville. The Methodist North Church was an antislavery church group, while the Methodist South organization was sympathetic to the Southern cause.

The first Congregational church organized in Santa Cruz in March 1852 was one of only four Congregational churches in California. In 1869 the Santa Cruz Congregational Church began an active Chinese Sunday School to convert immigrants who had recently come from China lured by the Gold Rush and prospects of economic prosperity. In 1881 the Congregational church expanded its Sunday School to a full Chinese Mission, and in 1892 the first Chinese Christian Society in the United States was formed here. While many Chinese remained tied to Confucianism, the Congregational church in Santa Cruz was extremely successful in its missionary work with this new group of industrious immigrants.

Above, left: As church membership grew in Santa Cruz County, touring evangelists began to make stops to address their respective congregations. The East Side Methodist Episcopal Church packed them in to hear "The Little Minister," a popular early twentieth-century evangelist. Courtesy, UCSC Special Collections

Above: In 1848 the Methodists became the first Protestant group organized in Santa Cruz County when Elihu Anthony founded a congregation in the city of Santa Cruz. Other Methodist congregations were soon begun. This circa-1900 illustration shows Watsonville's Methodist Episcopal Church, which was dedicated in 1874. It received extensive damage in the 1906 Earthquake. Courtesy, UCSC Special Collections

Right: The Joss House was a temple of worship for the immigrant Chinese community in Santa Cruz. Constructed of rough hewn redwood, as was typical of the structures in Chinatown, it was located in what would become a part of downtown Santa Cruz. Chinatown was destroyed by fire in 1887 and 1894. Courtesy, UCSC Special Collections

Above: This early photo shows the Santa Cruz Garfield Park Tabernacle. The structure was erected in 1890 and destroyed by fire in 1935. Courtesy, UCSC Special Collections

Following the Congregationalists, the Baptists (1858), Episcopalians (1862), and a Unity Church (1866) organized congregations in Santa Cruz County with other denominations following. By the turn of the century, over 20 Protestant churches had been built to house some 2,500 worshipers.

In 1906 a Watsonville Buddhist Temple was begun with over 200 members of primarily Japanese ancestry.

In addition to formal churches, the Santa Cruz area has long been a location for spiritual retreats.

In the late nineteenth century, areas such as Garfield Park in Santa Cruz were given to the State Association of Christian Churches with lots to be sold to members for permanent or summer cottages. Twin Lakes was donated to the Baptist Association in 1890, and Santa Maria del Mar was gifted to the Catholic Ladies' Aid Society in 1891 as a resort where "Catholic women of restricted means might go for periods of rest and recuperation." However, it was in 1905 that the full potential of Santa Cruz County as a religious retreat area began to materialize.

On December 12, 1905, the Mount Hermon Association was incorporated to manage a Christian conference center on Zayante Creek. That first summer season, some 2,000 people utilized the conference center and its grounds. As the forerunner of several such conference centers in Santa Cruz County, and as one of the first in California, Mount Hermon remains an important center for spiritual gatherings, as well as a center for group conferences. One of Mount Hermon's most noted guest speakers was the internationally recognized evangelist, Billy Graham, who in 1958 addressed followers at the center. Well into the 1980s, numerous retreats and religious

camps abound in the Santa Cruz Mountains and in Pajaro Valley, as well as the county's other popular areas.

The maturation and growth of governmental and religious institutions in Santa Cruz County paralleled, and perhaps necessitated, the growth of newspapers. Ideas preached from the pulpit and government regulations were scrutinized by the press. The ever-quickening pace of Yankee life required prompt dispersal of information to meet citizens' demands for timely information.

In 1855 in Monterey, John McElroy and Delos Ashly began a newspaper, the weekly *Monterey Sentinel.* On June 14, 1856, the paper moved to Santa Cruz to become the county's first newspaper. The *Pacific Sentinel,* as the paper was then called, cost its subscribers five dollars per year. The name was later changed to the *Sentinel,* the standard under which it still publishes. In 1884 the *Sentinel* changed from a weekly to a daily newspaper.

Duncan McPherson became affiliated with the *Sentinel* in 1864 and remained associated with it until his death in 1921. From 1921 until 1940, Fred D. McPherson, Duncan's son, took over where his father left off. After 1940 the younger McPherson's daughter and two sons acquired control of the *Sentinel.* The family has thus been involved with publishing the *Sentinel* since 1864, making it California's longest continuous newspaper dynasty.

By the turn of the century, Duncan McPherson had guided the *Sentinel* to a place of prominence in Santa Cruz—a niche the newspaper never relinquished. McPherson's contemporaries considered the *Sentinel* "indispensible to all," and a contribution to the "welfare and advancement of the county." Its descriptive articles were "of themselves a valuable history of the county." At times that history was not very attractive.

In his editorial columns, Duncan McPherson echoed the strong anti-Chinese immigrant sentiments persistent in Santa Cruz in the 1870s and 1880s. McPherson seemed to sincerely believe, as did the local citizenry who read his columns, that the Chinese immigrants were the scourge of society. With the possible exception of this period of bigotry, McPherson's record was one of responsibility which earned him the title "Dean of California's Newspaper Editors."

While the city of Santa Cruz harbored anti-Chinese sentiments, not all the county's communities vocalized such feelings. Watsonville, largely for economic reasons, defended the Chinese and was unusually sympathetic with their plight. This sympathy was evident in the local newspaper.

The Watsonville *Pajaronian* was first published in 1868. The Watsonville *Register,* which was also published during the late 1800s, was merged with the *Pajaronian* in 1913 to become the *Register-Pajaronian.* This Watsonville daily has the distinction of being the county's only newspaper to have been awarded a Pulitzer Prize.

Above: The Santa Cruz *Sentinel* is one of California's longest continually published newspapers. It achieved prominence in Santa Cruz in the nineteenth century, and remains the county's largest circulation daily. This photo illustrates the *Sentinel*'s bustling newsroom in the 1940s. Courtesy, UCSC Special Collections

Below: Ernest Otto was known as the "dean of Santa Cruz newspaper reporters." He went to work for the Santa Cruz *Sentinel* in 1919 and created a legacy of responsible reporting, a model emulated by many throughout California. Courtesy, UCSC Special Collections

"AS A CITY UPON A HILL"

Above: A.A. Taylor was editor of the Santa Cruz *Surf,* a popular newspaper of the day, until 1919 when the *Surf* was sold to the *Evening News* which later merged with the *Sentinel.* Taylor's pointed prose delighted readers and he became a well-known local personality. He was appointed by Governor Hiram Johnson to the California Redwood Park Commission, and also served as mayor of the city of Santa Cruz. Courtesy, UCSC Special Collections

In 1895 in Santa Cruz, the *Penny Press* was founded as an experiment to pioneer a one-cent daily. It was an immediate success, but economics eventually took their toll and the paper folded.

Numerous other Santa Cruz County newspapers have come and gone. Names such as the *Surf, Rustler, Courier, Transcript, Hatchet, Morning Sun, Mountain Echo, Local Item,* and *Daily Record* are now only memories. Two, however, deserve more mention due to the impact they had on their communities.

The Santa Cruz *Surf* opened its doors in 1883. It was edited by the charismatic A.A. Taylor. In his editorials, Taylor constantly demanded and supported civic responsibility. In one instance, in 1907, government scandal, occurring within California Redwood Park (Big Basin), was exposed in the *Surf.* Taylor had been a vocal supporter of the creation of California's first state park and was appointed to the California Redwood Park Commission to oversee its affairs.

In 1919 the *Surf* was sold to the *Evening News,* which later merged with the *Sentinel.*

The *Mountain Echo,* begun in 1896, was published in Boulder Creek in the upper San Lorenzo Valley every Saturday until 1917. The *Echo* dealt mainly with local news. Its editor, Winfield Scott Rodgers, constantly captivated and motivated his local readership.

Rodgers was born in 1853 and moved to Boulder Creek in 1874. He was elected to Boulder Creek's school board and served as a trustee for 70 years, making him the longest-serving school board member in California's history. He was also elected to the Santa Cruz County Board of Supervisors.

It is Rodgers' editorship of the *Mountain Echo* for which he is best remembered, however. After initial skepticism, he became an ardent supporter of the creation of a state park in Big Basin north of his home town of Boulder Creek. His rousing editorials stirred not only local action for the project, but support from surrounding communities as well. The creation of California Redwood Park at Big Basin in 1902 was due in part to Rodgers' personal efforts.

At one time, Rodgers was unable to procure newspaper stock. However, rather than let his readership do without, he printed the *Mountain Echo* on catalpa leaves. The citizens of Boulder Creek got their news on time!

The *Mountain Echo* stopped publishing in 1916, but Rodgers lived on to be 97 years old, and was able to witness the expansion and increasing public enjoyment of his beloved Big Basin Redwoods State Park.

With the opening of the University of California at Santa Cruz in 1965, several "free press" and alternative newspapers, as well as tourist tabloids, have been published in Santa Cruz County. While not yet attaining the circulation of the area's leading dailies, some of these papers have given independent writers the opportunity to

Top: As the communities of Santa Cruz and Watsonville grew, larger school buildings were constructed. Schools such as the Laurel School in Santa Cruz, shown here at the turn of the century, made one-room schoolhouses a memory of the past. Courtesy, UCSC Special Collections

Above: The Santa Cruz Free Library was organized in 1868, and was moved several times before it received its own permanent building in 1903-1904, as shown in the photo. In 1968 the current Santa Cruz Public Library replaced the original sandstone building and became the central branch of the modern multibranched city-county library system. Courtesy, Jennie and Denzil Verardo

Above: Winfield Scott Rodgers, editor of the *Mountain Echo*, is shown here on his ninetieth birthday. Courtesy, UCSC Special Collections

"AS A CITY UPON A HILL"

Above: The county's first schools, such as the Grant School in the city of Santa Cruz, were simple one-room buildings. Schooling dwelt on the basic three skills of reading, writing, and arithmetic. Prior to the establishment of the first public school, classes were held as early as 1848 in a private home. Courtesy, UCSC Special Collections

be published. They have also provided reader services not available elsewhere. Some periodicals, such as the university's own *City On A Hill Press,* have provided a valuable link with the educational community.

From the simple teachings of the Spanish fathers at Mission Santa Cruz, to the varied curriculum at the University of California, Santa Cruz County has long been associated with educational endeavors.

Prior to the establishment of the first public school, records show that Mrs. Mary Case opened a private school in her home in Santa Cruz in 1848. As early as 1853, Watsonville had a public school overseen by trustees selected by Judge John H. Watson.

In 1857 the first public school building in the county was erected in Santa Cruz. Mrs. Clara Adams was hired as the teacher at the rate of $50 a month. The county's school tax during those formative years was five cents on $100!

The growth rate of Santa Cruz was such that its one-room public school soon had to be expanded to two rooms. A tax was levied so a new two-room school could be built. In 1868 the structure was completed and by 1879, 10 teachers were employed in the Santa Cruz School District.

In 1857 the county's second school was opened in Pescadero, which was part of Santa Cruz County at that time. In 1868 the county line was adjusted and the area from Point Año Nuevo northward was transferred to San Mateo County.

Soon private and public schools, as well as public school districts, blossomed throughout the county. These included a school in

Watsonville for "colored citizens," who were not allowed to attend school with white children. The primary school for blacks, completed in 1867, had a teacher-student ratio of 1:18, whereas the school for whites had a ratio of 1:60!

In 1874 the California legislature ruled that non-white children could go to a white school if no colored school existed, and after 1875 mandated segregated education was brought to an end.

In 1861 Santa Cruz County had seven school districts. This soon increased to 37, and by 1892 there were 54 districts with 98 teachers. Commenting wth pride on the schools of Santa Cruz County, the superintendent of schools in 1890 stated that:

in no part of the State is the climate so well adapted to mental exertion. The mind is buoyant and active, and capable of great exertion with but little fatigue . . . Our county is so desireable as a place in which to establish homes . . . that we can always procure the best teachers without paying the highest salaries.

Many of the county's early schools were rural one-room schoolhouses. In 1896, 63 teachers taught in the county's country schools. These one-room facilities served the rural population well, even though many lacked lighting, running water, and most conveniences. "Where only the logger's axe breaks the silence, and beside the lonely mountain roads, perch the tiny schoolhouses, more than half a hundred of them, which are truly the temples of a new civilization." These country schools filled a valuable educational role by providing instruction close to home where children's labor was needed.

As more grammar schools were opened, the need for advanced schools was recognized. In 1876 Santa Cruz High School was built. A decade later, high school level classes began in Watsonville and in 1895 the Watsonville High School building was completed.

The parochial Holy Cross School in the city of Santa Cruz was founded in 1862 "for girls exclusively." It offered a curriculum which included high school courses. Aptos, Harbor (in Santa Cruz), and San Lorenzo Valley (Felton) high schools were later constructed to meet the ever-increasing need for high schools within the county.

On February 4, 1884, Santa Cruz County's first institution of higher learning, Chesnutwood's Business College, opened its doors. Founded by J.A. Chesnutwood, the school was a successful, coeducational business college that prepared students for "business life" through a self-paced course of study. The business college students came from several countries and other states, as well as from the local area, and it was the first college of its kind in California.

Cabrillo Junior College opened its doors in 1959 in Aptos, as part of California's Junior College System. With the renaming of the system, it became Cabrillo Community College.

No educational institution has made as great an impact on the

Above: Rural one-room schoolhouses were an important part of the county's educational system. Often lacking lighting and most other conveniences, these schools still served their population well. The Ben Lomond School was more elaborate than many of Santa Cruz County's rural schools. Over 50 such "temples of a new civilization" existed in the area. Courtesy, UCSC Special Collections

"AS A CITY UPON A HILL"

Above, right: In 1861 Santa Cruz County had seven school districts, but by the 1890s there were over 50 districts with close to 100 teachers. Within a short time, Santa Cruz went from a simple one-room schoolhouse to a multidistrict educational system that included schools with several stories and individual rooms. The variety of early Santa Cruz schools was depicted in an early work by Wallace Elliott & Co. From *Santa Cruz County, California,* 1879

Right: Founded in 1884, Chesnutwood's Business College was a successful private vocational college which solicited students through advertisements, such as this one, in magazines and newspapers. From Edward Harrison, *History of Santa Cruz County,* 1890

ADVERTISEMENTS.

The object of this College is to prepare young men and young ladies for the various business affairs of life. Its course is extensive, comprehensive, and practical, giving to all who graduate such a thorough business training as will fit them for *any business*. Its purpose is not *to fit pupils for clerks and book-keepers alone*, but aims to impart such information as will meet the wants of the times.

BOOK-KEEPING.
Our course in book-keeping is thorough and complete, embracing every kind of business, from the simplest transaction of the retail dealer to the complicated affairs of the most extensive foreign shipping houses.

BUSINESS CORRESPONDENCE
Will consist in writing business letters and communications of all kinds correctly.
The proper use of capitals; punctuation and phrasing will be thoroughly taught.
Penmanship in all its forms is made a specialty. All graduates will become elegant penmen.

COMMERCIAL LAW.
Lectures on Commercial Law will be given throughout the Business Course pertaining to business transactions and business paper.

MATHEMATICS.
A thorough drill will be given in Commercial Arithmetic, embracing the most rapid methods of calculating Fractions, Percentage, Interest, Discount, Partial Payments, Banking, Taxes, Insurance, Commission, Profit and Loss, Domestic and Foreign Exchange, Stocks, General Average, Partnership, Settlements, etc., embracing the principal business industries, such as Wholesale and Retail Merchandising, Railroading, Jobbing, Commission, Insurance, Farming, Brokerage, Banking, etc.

Terms, in advance: Full Business Course, including Penmanship, Six Months, $17. For further particulars call at the College Rooms, corner Pacific and Walnut Avenues, or address the Principal,

J. A. CHESNUTWOOD,
P. O. Box 43.   SANTA CRUZ, CAL.

SANTA CRUZ COUNTY

"AS A CITY UPON A HILL"

Designed by noted landscape architect Thomas Church, the campus structures of the University of California at Santa Cruz were designed to blend into their surroundings. When possible, redwood groves remained untouched as construction occurred. The campus is not scheduled for ultimate completion until the twenty-first century. Courtesy, UCSC Photo Lab

Each college at the University of California at Santa Cruz is both architecturally and academically unique. Undergraduates are assigned to a specific college within the university structure, and each college has a different academic focus. Based on the Oxford University system, students take basic courses within their specific college to maintain a "small school" atmosphere, while still having access to the larger centralized facilities such as the library, shown. Courtesy, UCSC Photo Lab

county as the University of California at Santa Cruz (UCSC). This impact would be felt socially, politically, and economically.

The California Constitution, drafted in 1849, provided for an educational system and a university. In 1868 the University of California was created by an act of the legislature with a single campus to be located in Berkeley. During the twentieth century, other campuses were added to the University of California in order to meet the state's increasing demand for higher education.

As part of the university's expansion program, three new campuses were authorized in 1957. Santa Cruz was chosen as the site for one of these. Two thousand acres were purchased from the S.H. Cowell Foundation in 1961, and in 1965 the University of California's Santa Cruz campus opened its doors.

The Santa Cruz campus plan is unique among those in the UC system. It is comprised of clusters of separate "colleges," similar to the system used at Oxford University in England. Each separate college has its own academic focus and student population. As the campus grows, new colleges are added. Central core facilities such as the library, laboratories, and administrative units are shared by all students. In this way the campus retains a small, personal atmosphere while still possessing the broad academic resources of the University of California.

Designed by Thomas Church, a renowned landscape architect, the campus blends creatively and sensitively into its spectacular environmental setting. Dean McHenry was appointed as the first chancellor and the "Santa Cruz Experience," unlike any other in the UC system, had begun.

In 1966 Lick Observatory, atop Santa Clara County's Mount Hamilton, became a part of the UCSC campus. James Lick had founded the world's first mountaintop observatory in 1875, and it had been transferred to the University of California system in 1888. Although the telescope itself remained on Mount Hamilton, over 60 tons of equipment were eventually transferred to the Santa Cruz campus where advanced astronomical research is now conducted.

In 1967, 86 students received their diplomas as UCSC's first graduating class. By 1986 over 7,000 undergraduates were enrolled in the "city upon a hill."

The growth and development of the University of California at Santa Cruz brought changes to both the city and county of Santa Cruz. Business boomed, and new enterprises catering to a growing population of students, faculty, and support personnel were established. The city of Santa Cruz, once considered a conservative resort and a retirement community, had to face the problems of skyrocketing property costs and changing social values. The once remote Spanish pueblo, having been transformed into a resort city, was now becoming a growing, restless, academic community. Only the paradisaical location remained the same.

SANTA CRUZ COUNTY

Frederick Hihn's Capitola Hotel was considered a first-class hotel at the turn of the century. Capitola's direct rail connection had ensured growth and frustrated nearby Soquel, which had been passed by. Courtesy, UCSC Special Collections

Chapter Four

BEYOND THE PUEBLO

Past the city limits of Santa Cruz lies an area rich in its land and lore.

To the north, up the coast, the scenery changes rapidly and drastically. Uplifted terraces are buffeted by the turbulent ocean that calms down as it rounds Lighthouse Point and becomes Monterey Bay. Without the sheltering effects of that bay, the north coast bears the brunt of ocean winds and fog. The storms are more severe, and living there demands a hardiness not required farther south.

At different times communities grew up along the north coast. One, Davenport Landing, was even considered a "boomtown."

In 1867 Captain John Pope Davenport, a whaler from Rhode Island, established headquarters for his whaling operations 12 miles north of Santa Cruz near the mouth of Agua Puerca Creek, and with John King built a 450-foot wharf. Davenport Landing soon became one of the major lumber shipping points on the coast, as well as a whaling center. During its boom years, the town boasted hotels, blacksmith shops, a store and hall, a shipyard, and the Agua Puerca School. Whaling in the area reached its peak around 1875, but prosperity in Davenport Landing continued into the 1880s. Then, as better shipping facilities were developed in other locations, the town began to decline. In the late 1880s Captain Davenport moved to Santa Cruz, where he was a real estate dealer and justice of the peace.

Lime from kilns three miles inland on San Vincente Creek continued to be shipped out at Davenport Landing until 1905. In 1906 owners of the Landing area sold their holdings to the newly incorporated Santa Cruz Portland Cement Company for $400,000. In 1907 the company constructed a cement plant about a mile south of Davenport Landing and helped usher in the new town of Davenport. That same year, the Coast Dairies and Land Company built a 28-room hotel to accommodate the factory's workers. The Ocean View Hotel would serve as a landmark in Davenport until 1962 when it was destroyed by fire.

Railroads further spurred the growth of this township. The ill-fated Ocean Shore Railroad had a line from Santa Cruz to north of Davenport. In November 1905 Southern Pacific secured right-of-way from Santa Cruz to Davenport and operated a line which added to the accessibility of this north coast town.

The cement plant was by far the leading source of commerce for the area, and for a time the development of Davenport kept pace with the expansion of the plant. In the 1920s a narrow-gauge electric railway was purchased by the company and moved down from Juneau, Alaska, to haul limestone to the plant from the inland quarry. And in 1934 the company erected a 2,327-foot wharf complete with pipes to transport the cement into the holds of waiting ships. Cement production reached 700,000 barrels a day after World War II, and the Davenport plant became one of the largest in the world.

Cement was not the only product of the north coast. Early on, logging was a major industry. Giant redwoods towered in many of the protected valleys. William Waddell recognized the value in this standing timber, as well as the advantage of having nearby ocean transportation. He already had a sawmill at Williams Landing, now the site of Davenport, as well as others at Rincon and Branciforte when, in 1862, he built his fourth mill in the valley which was given his name.

This mill and Waddell's home were situated at the confluence of East and West Waddell creeks. In order to connect with the nearest shipping point, Waddell in 1868 built a five-mile-long tramway from his mill to his wharf between Waddell Creek and Punta de Año Nuevo. For the next seven years, Waddell maintained an extensive lumber operation, and the small community of Seaside developed around the mill.

In 1875 Waddell received major injuries from a grizzly while bear hunting in the valley, and he died a short time later. Fire destroyed his mill, and storms eventually destroyed his wharf, but William Waddell is memorialized by the valley and creeks named after him.

As logging played out, farming became an important economic

Above: John Davenport brought his new wife back to California from Rhode Island in 1851. He ran a successful whaling operation and lumber wharf on the north coast at the landing named for him. Courtesy, Covello & Covello Photographers

Below: The cement plant built by the Santa Cruz Portland Cement Company at Davenport has been an industrial landmark on the north coast since its construction in 1907, when this picture was taken. It is now owned and operated by Lone Star Industries. Courtesy, Covello & Covello Photographers

BEYOND THE PUEBLO

Above: New crops were introduced to the north coast by immigrants who also brought cultural diversity and richness. The Italian artichoke growers shown here had proudly dressed up for this 1920s photo. Courtesy, Andy Ausonio

activity along the north coast. Dairying had begun well before the turn of the century and was joined by truck-farm crops of artichokes, broccoli, and brussels sprouts that were ideally suited to the fog-cooled climate. Farming continues to be of major importance to this area, although residential development seems to have become a real threat to it. One of the largest and most innovative of the north coast dairies recently passed through the hands of developers to became a state park—the Wilder Ranch.

Delos D. Wilder came to California from Connecticut in 1853. In 1871 Wilder and his family moved to Santa Cruz County, where he went into partnership with Levi K. Baldwin in a 4,030-acre dairy. The Baldwin and Wilder Dairy developed a reputation for making especially fine butter. In 1885 the partnership was dissolved and the land divided. Wilder received the "lower place" of 2,330 acres, and his share of the ranch's stock.

The Wilders continued to produce dairy products until 1930. New sanitation policies would have required the building of new facilities which, during the Depression, proved too expensive. Dairying continued until 1937, when the dairy herds were replaced by beef cattle.

When revenue from cattle and rodeo horse raising and income from leased-out ranch property failed to be enough to run the ranch and pay escalating taxes, the family had to sell off land. In 1969 the remaining ranch property was sold to a Canadian land development company, Moroto Investment Company, Ltd. It was slated to become a residential/commercial development with 33,000 residents.

The spirit, ingenuity, and effective utilization of resources that D.D. Wilder exemplified was evident in many early north coast settlers. But in the twentieth century the rural, agrarian economy has become harder to maintain. Rising taxes and ever-encroaching development have forced out long-established family operations. In a few fortunate areas, like Waddell's valley, now called Rancho del Oso, modern owners have valued preservation. There Theodore

Above: Farms and ranches like the Majors Ranch shown here in 1923 provided a new economic base for the area as logging and whaling played out. The bluffs are a characteristic feature of the north coast. Courtesy, Andy Ausonio

Above, left: An early 1900s camping party enjoys the beauty of the redwood forest in Big Basin north of Boulder Creek. Many areas like this were logged over in the lumber booms of the late nineteenth and early twentieth centuries. Courtesy, Jennie and Denzil Verardo

Hoover and his daughters maintained the area as a natural preserve until it finally became part of Big Basin Redwoods State Park. Challenges to the north coast continue and will determine its destiny.

Inland a few miles, separated from the rugged beauty of the north coast by the Santa Cruz Mountains, lies the verdant San Lorenzo Valley. Early descriptions tell of the San Lorenzo Valley being literally covered with giant redwoods. Settlement and development of the valley hinged on utilization of these trees.

As early as 1867, the county had recognized the need for services in the northern part of the valley and had laid out a road from the Ben Lomond area at Hick's Ford to the "forks of the San Lorenzo," located at the confluence of Bear Creek, Boulder Creek, and the San Lorenzo River. At that time, John Ellsworth had a mill operating nearby. A year later there were enough families in the area to necessitate a school, and the Boulder Creek School District was formed with one small building. In the early 1870s, a hotel, store, blacksmith shop, and post office were added to the new settlement.

Meanwhile, Joseph W. Peery had established his Silver Lumber Mills just south of Boulder Creek and by 1875 had begun the town of Lorenzo. Rivalry between the two towns began almost immediately. Peery had been the first postmaster at Boulder Creek and moved the post office to Lorenzo. A petition from Boulder Creek residents moved it back in the same year. Peery built a hotel in Lorenzo that was soon joined by a blacksmith shop and a store. When Boulder Creek residents erected the Washingtonian Hall "for purposes local, literary and social," Peery matched it by building a two-story Lorenzo Hall, and opened it with a gala Fourth of July celebration in 1877.

Although Lorenzo was able to secure a daily stage line to Santa Cruz, the railroad selected Boulder Creek as its final terminus. The South Pacific Coast Railroad laid out the new town of Boulder Creek

Right: Boulder Creek had a very active chapter of the Woman's Christian Temperance Union. Members are pictured here in front of their Free Reading Room circa 1900. The railroad had been "convinced" to donate the land for the building. Courtesy, UCSC Special Collections

Below, right: Boulder Creek, shown here at the turn of the century, became the dominant community over its rival Lorenzo when the railroad came through. The South Pacific Coast Railroad added the Town Park after its arrival in 1884. Courtesy, Jennie and Denzil Verardo

SANTA CRUZ COUNTY

Left: Henry L. Middleton's 45-acre estate, Madrone Villa, on Bear Creek Road just outside Boulder Creek, was considered one of the county's showplaces in the first decades of this century. Courtesy, UCSC Special Collections

Above: Rail service up the San Lorenzo Valley included a stop at Ben Lomond. Since the area's early economy was based on logging, the railroad proved a boon to development as well as to communication and travel. Courtesy, Covello & Covello Photographers

Left: Judge John Logan of Santa Cruz, who developed the Loganberry, laid out the town of Brookdale. Lying between Boulder Creek and Ben Lomond, it was famous for the Brookdale Lodge which had a creek running through its dining room. Courtesy, UCSC Special Collections

in 1884, and Lorenzo was eventually absorbed into it.

Logging had been the major activity in the Upper San Lorenzo Valley. By 1885 there were more than 20 sawmills working in the Boulder Creek area. The boom had begun in 1875, with the erection of the lumber flume from five miles north of Boulder Creek to Felton. The flume was replaced by a narrow-gauge railroad line which the Southern Pacific changed to standard gauge in 1907 to meet operational demands. The Boulder Creek Hotel was expanded, the McAbee brothers moved their livery stables over from Lorenzo, and a butcher shop and store were all signs of increased prosperity for Boulder Creek.

Henry L. Middleton, who would become one of the leading citizens of Boulder Creek, opened the Big Basin Mercantile Company in partnership with the Cunninghams. Middleton would also own the California Timber Company, the Boulder Creek Land and Timber Company, the Western Shore Lumber Company, and the Santa Clara Valley Mill and Lumber Company. He was instrumental in bringing new inventions like electric lighting to Boulder Creek and was an active booster for the area. While making his fortune in the logging and lumber business, Middleton also possessed a sensitivity to the need for preservation of redwoods for future generations. He aided in the establishment of the state park in Big Basin, and his company donated 1,300 acres of adjoining cutover property to round out the park's initial boundaries. He later served as a vice president of the Sempervirens Club, the conservation group that had initiated the park idea. Middleton was also appointed by the governor in 1911 to serve on the California Redwood Park Commission. When he died in 1930, H.L. Middleton left a large personal estate and a permanent imprint on the Upper San Lorenzo Valley.

Middleton was one of a number of successful lumbermen in the area. At one time there were, within a seven-mile radius of Boulder Creek, some 50 saw and shingle mills in operation. But the resource was soon depleted. By 1934 mills were closed and the railroad to Felton shut down. Tracks were torn up, and Boulder Creek was forced to find a new way to make a living. In recent years tourism has become a dominant economic activity.

Down-valley from Boulder Creek is the town of Ben Lomond. It too began with a sawmill and was dependent on logging for its economy.

One of Ben Lomond's earliest settlers was Captain Harry Love. In 1855 Love moved to the San Lorenzo Valley and married the widowed mother of Jackson and Winston Bennett. The Bennetts had established a sawmill in the area in 1848. Love logged the area and gave his name to the creek which fed the mill. In 1868 Harry Love was killed by Chris Iverson, another Santa Cruz Mountain resident, in a shooting in Santa Clara.

In that same year, new residents were added to the Love Creek

Left: **The Howden Castle, a Ben Lomond landmark since the early 1900s, has always been a private residence. Courtesy, UCSC Special Collections**

region. Napoleon Bonaparte Hicks built a home and a sawmill south of Love's mill. He was joined for a time by his brother, Achilles Scipio Hicks. James Priest, who had married Love's stepdaughter, settled north of the mill. James Pierce of Santa Clara purchased the Hicks property and established the Pacific Manufacturing Company there. Pierce and his superintendent, Thomas L. Bell, laid out the town in 1888, and the local school became the Pacific Mills School. The town was named after a nearby peak which Thomas Burns, a Scotsman, had christened "Ben Lomond Mountain."

Burns had come to the area in the 1850s, and with I.C. Willson put in the county's first vineyard beyond the old mission. The Ben Lomond Winery came into the ownership of F.W. Billings and John Q. Packard after Burns' death in 1880. Billings' son-in-law John F. Coope was made superintendent and general manager, and he intro-

Above: The city of Santa Cruz, with Monterey Bay in the distance, does indeed look like paradise. Courtesy, Alexander Lowry

Right: Sailing is another popular activity in Santa Cruz County. Courtesy, Alexander Lowry

Above: Capitola's beach has long been a popular area for young and old alike. Courtesy, Alexander Lowry

Left: Surfing is a popular sport along the Santa Cruz Coast. Courtesy, Alexander Lowry

Right: The Santa Cruz Lighthouse is a museum dedicated to the sport of surfing. Courtesy, Alexander Lowry

Above: The art of pruning is demonstrated by a worker at the Felton-Empire Vineyards. Courtesy, Alexander Lowry

Top right: The town of Boulder Creek in the upper San Lorenzo Valley has changed little since the turn of the century. Courtesy, Alexander Lowry

Middle right: Apples have always been Watsonville's claim to fame in agriculture. Watsonville apples and apple juice are known and shipped around the world. Courtesy, Alexander Lowry

Right: Along with apples, row crops such as lettuce play a major role in the local economy. The fertile Pajaro Valley has been used for agriculture since the days of the Spanish missions. Courtesy, Alexander Lowry

62

Above: As popular as ever, the Santa Cruz Beach and Boardwalk is one of the area's major tourist attractions, and has been for decades. Courtesy, Alexander Lowry

Left: A sculpture and students on UCSC's grounds are silhouetted in the fading light. Courtesy, Alexander Lowry

Above: The roller coaster at the Santa Cruz Boardwalk is one of the few remaining traditional roller coasters in the United States. Courtesy, Alexander Lowry

BEYOND THE PUEBLO

duced machinery to the processes in the vineyard and in the winery. The winery won prizes in competitions in Paris and was praised by the German Royal Viticulture Commission.

As logging declined, so did the fortunes of Ben Lomond. Tourism—centered around Thomas Bell's Rowardennan Hotel—became the new focus when farming proved unprofitable.

The southern portion of the San Lorenzo Valley had originally been part of two Spanish land grants, Rancho Zayante and Rancho Rincon. On a portion of Rancho Zayante, Edward Stanley laid out a town in 1868. Named by Stanley after his attorney, future-Senator Charles N. Felton, this community had already been a lumbering center for more than two decades.

After Felton was laid out, Stanley and Eben Bennett began work to connect the area to Santa Cruz. There had been a road constructed from Santa Cruz north to the Rincon, and the road down had been completed as far as Gold Gulch. When the connecting link was finished, it operated as a toll road until it was paid for in 1872.

By the early 1870s, Felton was becoming a prosperous community. The town would soon boast three hotels, a depot, a church, a saloon, a "flourishing school," a post office, livery stables, and a blacksmith shop, as well as a public hall. Built in 1876, the lumber flume from up-valley terminated just south of town and provided jobs transferring lumber from the flume pond to waiting railroad cars for the trip down to Santa Cruz.

In 1884 the South Pacific Coast Railroad completed a line up the valley to Boulder Creek which became the new center for lumber shipping in the valley. The lumber flume was now obsolete and was soon dismantled. Felton was slowed, but not stopped. In 1892 a new covered bridge was built across the San Lorenzo assuring travel down to Santa Cruz. Although the town was nearly destroyed by fire in 1888 and again in 1896, the plucky residents rebuilt and carried on. As early as 1896, it was noted that "the village counts so safely on a large contingent of summer-comers that a regular business is made of providing for their needs, their pleasures, and even their whims."

Beyond the reaches of the San Lorenzo River, the Santa Cruz Mountains have harbored several other communities. For most of these towns, the end of lumbering as a substantial industry was the harbinger of their decline. One in particular, however, went through a decline to rebound even stronger.

Scotts Valley was part of a Spanish land grant that was used during the mission period for grazing, and later was known for its grain crops and dairies and its orchards and vineyards. It, too, declined, mainly because it did not possess timber during the logging boom. Since the 1960s, however, Scotts Valley has become one of the fastest growing areas in the county. Its accessibility to the Santa Clara Valley has allowed its development as a suburban community and as a location for high-tech research and development facilities.

Above: Isaac Graham, one of the most conspicuous of the early American settlers in Santa Cruz County, once held the land which Felton grew up on as part of his Rancho Zayante. His name remains on one of the main roads from Santa Cruz to Felton. Courtesy, Jennie and Denzil Verardo

Left: The restless sea, shown here at West Cliff Drive, is evident everywhere along the Santa Cruz County coast. Sightseers and residents alike enjoy this spectacular attraction. Courtesy, Alexander Lowry

Below: Felton's Grand Central Hotel began life in the early 1880s as Thomas Cramer's Central Hotel. A fire in 1888, a few years before this picture was taken, leveled much of the business section, but Felton residents quickly rebuilt. Courtesy, UCSC Special Collections

The San Lorenzo Valley did not possess all of the timber in Santa Cruz County. Several mid-county communities also began life as lumber towns. Logging in the Soquel area began in the 1840s. Michael and Martina Castro Lodge built a sawmill on Soquel Creek in 1845. Over the next decade, their sawmill would be joined by those of John Daubenbiss and John Hames, Gervis Hammond and Hugh McCall, Gershal Kirby, Roger Hinckley and John Shelby, Benjamin Cahoon, Lansing Haight, and the Grovers. Joel Bates added innovation with his construction of a steam-powered mill on Bates Creek in 1857.

In addition to lumbering, the Soquel area also supported flour mills to process the wheat which was grown from the Pajaro Valley up to Santa Cruz. To handle the lumber, food, and manufactured items that were being produced nearby, a wharf was built at Soquel Landing west of the mouth of Soquel Creek in 1857.

Soquel grew so quickly that just eight years after its founding as a township in 1852, it was the third largest settlement in the county. C.K. and B.F. Porter established a tannery nearby in 1853, which was soon turning out 25,000 tanned hides annually. In 1858 the Santa Clara Turnpike Company completed its road that connected Santa Cruz and Santa Clara counties. The road ran just west of Soquel Creek and helped spur further growth in this area. A paper mill built by the O'Neill brothers in 1879 added more diversity to the local community and was in business until the 1920s.

One of Soquel's largest concerns in the 1870s was the sugar refinery of W.T. Garrat and Associates, known as the California Sugar Beet Company. Utilizing sugar beets grown nearby and in the Pajaro Valley, the wood-fueled plant operated from 1874-1879. It did not achieve real success, however, because the 50-ton-capacity mill proved too small to be operated profitably.

Soquel made an unsuccessful bid to become the county seat, and in 1868 the town even attempted to become the state capital. A movement had begun to move the capital out of Sacramento, and Soquel residents, probably supported by the influential Frederick A. Hihn, proposed building a town hall and inviting the state legislature to use it. If Hihn was involved, it may have been the only time he was not successful in this vicinity.

Frederick Hihn had begun his involvement in the county in the city of Santa Cruz. Successful in his retail and real estate activities there, he expanded southward by acquiring a large portion of land in the valley of Soquel Creek. Logging operations on this property were so intense that Hihn's mill at Laurel produced 50,000 board feet of lumber a day from timber cut on Soquel and Laurel creeks.

On the coast, Hihn expanded the Soquel Landing wharf and began to make plans for the resort he dubbed Camp Capitola. Beginning in 1869 with a camping area on Soquel Creek, Hihn eventually built up his resort to include a hotel with accommodations for over

BEYOND THE PUEBLO

Left: Beginning in 1884, Frederick Hihn sold lots at Camp Capitola. These residential lots ranged in price from $100 to $300. His corporation owned parks like this one, plus all the streets, bridges, waterlines, and sewers. In 1937 it was all deeded to the county. Courtesy, Jennie and Denzil Verardo

Right: Five years after its incorporation in 1949, the City of Capitola hosted its first Begonia Festival. Billing itself as Begonia Capital, the city's festivities included a parade of flower-bedecked "floats" down Soquel Creek. Courtesy, UCSC Special Collections

Below: Constructed of cement for use as a U.S. navy tanker during World War I, the *Palo Alto* was finally moved down to Seacliff Beach near Aptos in 1929. A pier was constructed out to where the ship was grounded. Until a storm cracked the hull in 1932, it was used as an amusement and fishing ship. Courtesy, Jennie and Denzil Verardo

100 guests, a dining room, bathhouse, and private beach. With the completion of the Santa Cruz-Watsonville Railroad by Hihn and Claus Spreckels in 1876, the success of Camp Capitola seemed assured. The line had a stop in Capitola, but bypassed Soquel, causing hard feelings in that proud community.

By 1894 Hihn was building a new, larger Capitola Hotel. His three-story hotel opened in 1895. At that time Capitola was described as "the gem of the Bay of Monterey" and Hihn's resort called "one of the most popular seaside resorts in California." In 1904 Fred Swanton's Santa Cruz Capitola and Watsonville Railway brought electric rail service to Capitola and made it even more accessible.

Nearby in Aptos another successful businessman was constructing a resort which was modeled after Hihn's. Claus Spreckels not only built the Aptos Hotel but became one of Aptos' most illustrious citizens.

Spreckels' 2,390-acre holdings had been part of Rancho Aptos which was granted to Rafael Castro in 1833. Two decades before Spreckels' arrival, a sawmill erected on Aptos Creek in 1851 had been the beginning of the major industry for this community. By the 1880s activity in the timber industry was brisk, and most of the redwood around Aptos was being cut.

Second generations of pioneer families played a big part in the development of Aptos, with José Arano, son-in-law of Rafael Castro,

67

operating a store and acting as postmaster, and Isaac Graham's son-in-law, David Rice, establishing a hotel. In 1860 the county erected a bridge across the creek and made travel to and through Aptos much easier. And in 1871 a school was built on land donated by Rafael Castro. Most of the early settlement had been on the west side of Aptos Creek, but by the 1870s development was progressing on both sides.

Spreckels had built his Aptos Hotel for his personal guests soon after purchasing the property from Castro in 1872. Many of the dignitaries and luminaries of that day were entertained by Claus Spreckels, including King Kalakaua of Hawaii who visited Aptos in 1881. Spreckels not only enlarged the wharf at Aptos to accommodate schooners carrying lumber to Hawaii, but gave a further boost to the logging industry through the Santa Cruz-Watsonville Railroad he built with Hihn. Spreckels provided right-of-way over his property, and Aptos soon became a lumber center. But it was the Pajaro Valley that was destined to feel the impact of Claus Spreckels more than any other part of the county.

From its beginnings, development of the Pajaro Valley centered on agriculture. With the coming of American settlers, former rancho pastureland was placed under cultivation. Early crops included barley, wheat, and potatoes. In the late 1820s, Captain John Cooper had erected a small gristmill on Rancho Bolsa del Pajaro where Watsonville is now located. (Several explanations for the name Watsonville exist, including the fact that there were three men in town with the surname Watson.) Grain continued as the valley's major crop for many years, feeding nearby gristmills and, later, paper mills.

In 1853, the same year that a potato "glut" threatened to ruin many local farmers, Jesse D. Carr planted the area's first orchard. He was joined the next year by William White. By 1858 commercial orchards were being planted. Those of Judge Peckham and Isaac Williams joined earlier orchards in what would become a mainstay of agricultural production in the area. In 1861 James Waters increased orchard acreage tremendously when he set out 2,000 trees, almost all apple, east of the Pajaro Valley Orphan Asylum. Soon other crops—including blackberries, strawberries, currants, apricots, and pears—were added. Wheat remained the dominant crop but the apple industry was growing every year.

In 1868 Stephen Martinelli established Martinelli's Cider and Soda Works in Watsonville. He had come to California from Switzerland in 1859 and eventually settled in the Pajaro Valley near his brother Louis. He soon realized that the apple cider that was available was of less-than-adequate quality. Martinelli felt that he could improve on the product, and he certainly did! Martinelli's cider has won many gold and silver medals in competitions, and today the business is the second oldest in Watsonville.

The distinction of being the oldest business in Watsonville belongs to the Charles Ford Company. Charles Ford moved to the Pajaro Valley in 1852, where he first planted potatoes on land leased from the Amesti family. Later he opened a store with Lucius Sanborn. He and Sanborn went on to form the Watsonville Mill and Lumber Company with logging operations near Corralitos. Both enterprises proved profitable, and in the 1860s Ford opened branch stores in Monterey County. When Sanborn retired, A.A. Morey and James S. Menasco became Ford's partners.

Charles Ford also invested in real estate, to the extent that he is credited with owning one-fourth of the property that the town of Watsonville occupied. In addition to being the principal organizer and first president of the Bank of Watsonville, Ford in 1860 began his one term in the state assembly. Ford never married, and when he died he left a personal estate valued at $300,000 which was distributed primarily to his family in the East. Ford's Department Store in Watsonville is still located at the same place that Ford and Sanborn had their first store.

In 1872 the Southern Pacific extended its rail lines from Gilroy to Pajaro across the river from Watsonville. While residents of Watsonville were disappointed that they did not get a direct rail connection, they soon wore deep ruts in the road to Pajaro with wagon-loads of products for rail distribution. In 1876 rail service from Santa Cruz did connect directly with Watsonville and helped strengthen ties with the rest of the county.

The new narrow gauge to Santa Cruz helped to transport lumber from the Corralitos area, as well as sugar beets from the Pajaro Valley to the California Sugar Beet plant at Soquel. That plant proved unprofitable, but with the entrance of Claus Spreckels, sugar beets were to become a valuable crop in the Pajaro Valley.

Spreckels had become interested in the use of sugar beets for refining after working as a common laborer in a German beet sugar mill in 1865. Returning to California, he organized the California Sugar Refinery. It wasn't yet economical to use beets, so Spreckels imported cane from the Philippines, China, Java, and Hawaii.

Spreckels, having established very close ties with Hawaiian King Kalakaua, controlled enough sugar cane plantations there to be considered the Sugar King of Hawaii. But by the fall of 1886, Claus Spreckels' political influence in Hawaii had waned and he was facing possible hostility from restive native growers. He had done some experimenting with sugar beet production at his Aptos Ranch, and now the time was right to turn to beets.

Claus Spreckels approached several communities with the proposal to locate his refinery there, including Antioch, Santa Maria, and Watsonville. He had two stipulations which had to be met. One was that the farmers of the area would guarantee to plant and grow at least 2,000 acres of sugar beets each year, utilizing the German methods of crop rotation and fertilization. The second was that the

Left: The Apple Annual—"an apple show where apples grow"—was held in Watsonville from 1910 until 1914 when it was moved to San Francisco. The event featured spectacular displays made from apples. Courtesy, UCSC Special Collections

Above: The home of the Apple Annual was a popularly subscribed building designed by W.H. Weeks. For the 1910 annual, Fred Swanton loaned tents to hold the overflow. The Watsonville Fire Station now occupies this site. Courtesy, Pajaro Valley Historical Association

Left: By 1912 the Apple Annual was such a success that it attracted two U.S. navy submarines. Unfortunately, while anchored off Port Watsonville, the anchor cable snapped on one of them and it ran aground, with the subsequent loss of two lives. Courtesy, the Pat Hathaway Collection

community selected would donate the factory site.

After Spreckels spoke to a gathering in Watsonville in November 1887, a committee composed of Charles Ford, William Gaffey, and W.R. Ratcliffe was appointed to select a site. A 25-acre parcel on Walker Street was agreed upon, and its $14,000 cost was to be paid by public subscription. A total of 240 pledges were made. When it was recognized that all of the money would not be available in time, Ford provided a loan for the difference. The largest contributor was Charles Ford, followed by Frederick Hihn. Contributions ranged from $1,000 down to $10. A total of $950 was donated by Santa Cruz residents in a strong show of support for their southern neighbor.

In April 1888 the factory's cornerstone was laid. That fall the plant, equipped with machinery Spreckels had shipped from Germany, began operation. The first season saw the new factory processing 350 tons of beets per day into 40 tons of raw sugar.

For a decade Watsonville grew and prospered. In the first year, the plant processed 2,920,000 pounds of beets. In 1892 its capacity was increased from 350 to 700 tons a day, and then to 1,000 tons a day. It employed 300 workers at the plant, and dozens of farmers made their living by raising sugar beets.

But, as the factory expanded, more beet acreage had to be found, and the same year the plant capacity was increased the Western Sugar Beet Company leased 600 acres near Castroville in Monterey County. The Pajaro Valley Railroad (built by Spreckels) was utilized to bring the beets to the plant at Watsonville. But as beet acreage in the Castroville area and in the Salinas Valley increased, this shipment became increasingly unfeasible.

In 1899 Spreckels completed a larger plant near Salinas in Monterey County. The new plant in a town christened "Spreckels" had a capacity of 3,000 tons a day that was more than that of all of the other beet plants in California combined. Spreckels' factory in Watsonville was closed down and dismantled but, to the chagrin of locals, the land was not returned.

Watsonville's sugar prosperity ended almost as quickly as it had begun, but by this time the town was well-established and not ready to give up! Apples had become the dominant crop, replacing wheat and hops which had been key agricultural commodities for the valley during the 1880s and 1890s. By 1909 there were one million apple trees planted on over 14,000 acres of the Pajaro Valley, producing about three million boxes of apples.

Another crop important to the valley was introduced in 1914 when Moses Hutchings planted three acres of lettuce. From that small, determined start, the Watsonville lettuce industry grew to ship 304 railroad carloads in 1922. By 1951 the Pajaro Valley was providing its share of the 33,203 carloads of lettuce shipped from the Salinas-Watsonville area. And once again, dependence on agricultural commodities proved beneficial to the south county area.

SANTA CRUZ COUNTY

In 1916 National Guard Company L from Watsonville was sent to guard the U.S.-Mexican border from the raids of Pancho Villa. Here members of Company L walk down Watsonville's main street as they prepare to depart for the border town of Nogales, Arizona. They returned home only to face the mobilization of World War I. Courtesy, Pajaro Valley Historical Association

Chapter Five

PRIDE, PREJUDICE, AND PROTEST

By the twentieth century, many patterns had been delineated on the Santa Cruz County landscape. Principal communities had been established, tourism had become a potent economic activity, and conservation forces were successful in setting aside tracts of unspoiled parkland.

Literary and artistic foundations were also being established which would enhance the area's recognition and contribute to the pride of its citizenry. In the 1860s, while vacationing in Santa Cruz, Bret Harte penned *The Luck of Roaring Camp.* At the time, Harte was also the editor of a newly founded San Francisco literary magazine, *Overland.* This publication has been said to have given birth to true "California" literature.

Josephine Clifford McCrackin was not only a contributor to *Overland,* but became Harte's assistant. While Harte's influence on McCrackin is obvious in her use of western settings for her stories, the Santa Cruz County writer introduced a social aspect in her writing which was unique for that era. Drawing from her tragic personal life, McCrackin often depicted her characters as women who, separated from their husbands, were forced to earn a living in a society which distrusted female independence. She soon became widely known and read in literary circles and formed associations with some of the foremost authors of that day.

One prominent literary figure in particular, Ambrose Bierce, became a familiar face in the county through his friendship with Josephine McCrackin. Bierce had a clever and irreverent writing style, and the restlessness of his life challenged the places he chose to live and the company he kept. Vacationing even in this paradise was not enough to quell the despair and anxiety which pervaded his life, however. In 1913 Bierce left for Mexico to join Pancho Villa's revolution. In 1914 Bierce was killed as he deserted Villa's cause.

Josephine Clifford McCrackin moved to the city of Santa Cruz after her home at Wrights was destroyed by fire. For many years she was a noted journalist with the *Sentinel.* She is particularly remembered for her scathing attacks on local lumber interests and for her call to "Save the Redwoods." By her death in 1920 at age 82, Josephine Clifford McCrackin had been instrumental in the redwood forest preservation movement, as well as having been the founding president of the Ladies Forest and Songbird Protective Association, honorary vice president of the California Audubon Society, and a member of the California Fish Protective Association.

Georgianna Bruce Kirby was another writer who called Santa Cruz "home." Kirby had been acquainted with Ralph Waldo Emerson and Henry David Thoreau through her connections with the Transcendentalist movement and such social experiments as Brook Farm. Her *Years of Experience* had a profound influence on those connected with the social reform movement throughout the United States. She moved to the Santa Cruz area in 1852 as an established author and activist and continued her work here.

The strong literary tradition established in Santa Cruz County in the nineteenth century has carried through into the twentieth century. One of the most dynamic and exciting modern writers was H.A. Van Coenen Torchiana. His *History of Mission Santa Cruz,* published in 1933, remains the most comprehensive reference on the subject.

James D. Houston's *The Californians* delivers a cross section of the state's cultures and lifestyles and has received critical acclaim for this local resident. *Farewell to Manzanar,* which he coauthored with Jeanne Wakatsuki Houston, was recognized as one of the most factual and sensitive portrayals of the World War II Japanese internment.

Page Smith, professor emeritus at UCSC and county resident, earned the reputation of being one of the most respected American historians and also one of the most prolific. His *John Adams* is considered the definitive work on the statesman. *The Historian and History* remains a classic of modern historical theory, and Smith's multivolume *Redeeming the Time,* published in 1986, has been called a "masterwork."

Above: Josephine Clifford McCrackin, shown here circa 1910, was a member of Bret Harte's "Overland School" of writers. She received numerous honors before her death in 1920, including the declaration of Josephine Clifford McCrackin Day at the 1916 San Diego Exposition. Courtesy, UCSC Special Collections

PRIDE, PREJUDICE, AND PROTEST

The county has had its share of painters, also. In 1856 the artist Leon Trousset painted one of the earliest oils of Santa Cruz. Trousset traveled throughout California leaving works that are considered masterpieces of that period.

Local artist Frank Heath's 1893 *Birdseye View of Santa Cruz* hung at the 1933-1934 Chicago World's Fair, and his oil paintings were shown at the St. Louis World's Fair. Heath exhibited in many cities across the country and attained a respected status in the world of art. He had studied at Mark Hopkins Art Institute in San Francisco and taught there for a decade before moving to Santa Cruz to open a studio. Frank Heath was a charter member of the Santa Cruz Art League which was formed in 1919, and served as its first president.

In another artistic medium, Andrew Hill's studio in Big Basin served as a base for his spectacular redwood photographs. One of his works, a panorama of 13 photos—which when combined measured 22 inches high and 17 feet long—was the largest scenic piece taken until that time. It was displayed at the Pan-American Exposition in Buffalo, New York, in 1901, where it created a sensation by affording Easterners a seldom-seen view of the spectacular coast redwoods of Santa Cruz County.

In the field of architecture, William Weeks stands out. Weeks moved to Watsonville in 1892 to design a building for the Christian Church. By his death in 1936, he had designed numerous churches, as well as banks and libraries, private residences and commercial buildings, and over 1,200 schools throughout California. William Weeks is considered one of the state's most influential architects, and many of his designs remain as beautiful and useful buildings in Santa Cruz County.

The real beginning of theatrical arts in the area was in 1877 when the Opera House was completed in Santa Cruz. It played host to future stage and screen star Zasu Pitts who got her start there. The Opera House also boasted appearances by General Tom Thumb, the internationally famous midget from P.T. Barnum's show; Jack London, the renowned Socialist author; and Thomas Nast, one of the nation's first political cartoonists. Although the Opera House was torn down in 1961, its theater arts legacy remains in several locations in the county.

Santa Cruz County citizens have also distinguished themselves in politics. In 1855 William W. Stow became the first county resident to serve as speaker of the California assembly. Stow gained notoriety because of his relationship with Colis P. Huntington and the skillful machinations he performed for Southern Pacific Railroad. Benjamin Knight became the first county representative to serve as president pro tempore of the state senate when he assumed that position in 1885.

William T. Jeter of Santa Cruz served as lieutenant governor of California from 1895 to 1899. Santa Cruz residents witnessed the

Below: During this Native Sons of the Golden West Convention in Santa Cruz in the late 1880s, political and patriotic banners hung for all to see. The view looks north on Pacific Avenue. Courtesy, UCSC Special Collections

75

procession of dignitaries visiting Jeter's Beach Hill home. He was also president of the County Bank of Santa Cruz for 37 years. Until his death at 80 in 1930, William Jeter remained an active member of the local community, constantly promoting the public good.

Santa Cruz Sentinel publisher Duncan McPherson was one of the area's most influential personalities at the turn of the century. Even though he considered himself a Republican, McPherson's actions were well-suited to the Populist philosophies. Major campaign planks for the Populists—who considered themselves reform-minded—included women's suffrage and the demand for prohibition of all Oriental immigration.

During this same period, women's suffrage activist Susan B. Anthony visited Santa Cruz. Though this was her second visit, she received a great deal more local support this time, including McPherson's public endorsement.

During the first decade of the twentieth century, the county was the subject of numerous magazine articles which touted its paradisaical qualities. The national attention focusing on the merits of Santa Cruz's ideal tourist setting, as well as the strong conservation sentiments embodied in the area's citizenry, played no small part in the decision by President Theodore Roosevelt to visit the area in 1903.

In 1906 the Republicans chose Santa Cruz for their state convention, and again political attention turned to this area. The convention was held in huge tents as Fred Swanton's famous casino and resort, which was to host the Republicans, had just burned down. At the meeting itself, James Gillette was chosen as the party's candidate for governor, over incumbent Republican Governor George Pardee. The state's railroad-controlled "bosses" did not want Pardee reelected because of his refusal to be influenced or intimidated by the Southern Pacific.

Ironically, some anti-Southern Pacific interests did not want Pardee reelected either. He had alienated a powerful group of Republican politicos during the previous gubernatorial election when he thwarted their candidate's bid for the governorship. Representing this group at Santa Cruz was Warren Porter who delivered 36 anti-Pardee delegates to Gillette and was then unanimously selected by the convention to be the Republican candidate for lieutenant governor.

Both James Gillette and Warren Porter won the state election in 1906, and Santa Cruz County, for the second time in a decade, was home to a lieutenant governor. Statewide results showed that Gillette polled fewer votes than any other candidate on the Republican ticket, and the controversy surrounding his selection at the Santa Cruz Republican Convention contributed to that result. In 1907 legislation requiring direct primaries was passed, and so the 1906 Santa Cruz Convention became one of the last state nominating conventions held in California.

While the political activity of 1906 was significant to the county,

Above: William Jeter, one of Santa Cruz County's foremost citizens, was well respected throughout California as well as by his local community. Jeter served as lieutenant governor of California from 1895-1899, and as president of the County Bank of Santa Cruz from 1893 until his death in 1930. Courtesy, UCSC Special Collections

Above, right: In 1902 Governor Henry T. Gage visited Santa Cruz County's famous California Redwood Park at Big Basin. Governor Gage had signed the bill into law which created California's first state park despite strong political pressure to do otherwise. Courtesy, the Sempervirens Fund

Right: While earthquakes have caused damage to Santa Cruz County, periodic flooding has been both more prevalent and more destructive. The 1911 flood, shown here, caused severe property damage. Previous floods had occurred in 1852, 1862, and 1907. Courtesy, Jennie and Denzil Verardo

other events occurred which would also occupy local attention.

On April 18, 1906, the Great Earthquake struck, causing considerable damage and destruction throughout Santa Cruz County. Numerous commercial buildings as well as homes, bridges, and roads were damaged. Fire-fighting equipment was kept outside for fear that aftershocks would bring down the fire department's buildings. Clean-up and rebuilding would occupy county residents for many months.

Previous earthquakes in 1865 and 1868 had caused damage in the county. According to Warren Porter who experienced both the 1868 and the 1906 earthquakes, the later tremor was "no worse than the one of 1868."

After the disaster, the county's lime and cement industries experienced a brief boom. Limekilns worked at capacity as demand for cement rose to supply the reconstruction efforts. The average combined monthly output of the county's three largest lime and cement companies had been 20,000 barrels. After the earthquake, the Henry

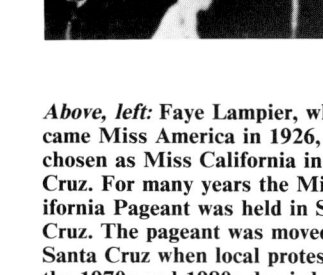

Cowell Lime and Cement Company alone sold 17,000 barrels of lime in one week. Ironically, the earthquake also generated the eventual decline of the lime industry as demand diminished for brick houses, which could not survive temblors.

Two years after the earthquake, President Theodore Roosevelt's Great White Fleet of 16 battleships steamed across Monterey Bay on its way to Santa Cruz, and local citizens poured out to see the event.

Never before had Santa Cruz County witnessed such a spectacle. A local newspaper reported that "It was imposing almost to the point of awe" for area residents, and they flocked to see the ships whose 12-inch guns could "hurl a half-ton projectile of solid steel through every building in Watsonville." After the ships docked in Santa Cruz, schoolchildren were given tours of Uncle Sam's fleet, and sailors were treated to a "monster barbeque dinner" by the proud

Above, left: **Faye Lampier, who became Miss America in 1926, was chosen as Miss California in Santa Cruz. For many years the Miss California Pageant was held in Santa Cruz. The pageant was moved from Santa Cruz when local protests in the 1970s and 1980s decried the image of women it portrayed. Courtesy, Jennie and Denzil Verardo**

Above: **In 1903 President Theodore Roosevelt visited Santa Cruz and commented on the need to preserve the area's redwoods. On May 11, 1903, the Roosevelt Tree in what is now Henry Cowell Redwoods State Park was dedicated in his honor. Courtesy, Jennie and Denzil Verardo**

PRIDE, PREJUDICE, AND PROTEST

Above, right: In 1908 President Theodore Roosevelt's Great White Fleet of battleships visited Santa Cruz. Citizens poured out to see the might of Uncle Sam's modern navy. After World War I, the Pacific Fleet again visited Santa Cruz, when this photograph was taken. Courtesy, UCSC Special Collections

local citizenry.

With the outbreak of World War I in August 1914, however, harsh descriptions of battles replaced the metaphoric pride in the floating instruments of war. The "War to end all Wars" became even more real and personal with America's entry into the conflict in 1917. When the draft board met at Army Hall in Santa Cruz on August 7, 1917, local citizens were brought face-to-face with the realities of war as 94 recruits were selected to make up the county's first draft contingent.

In 1916 National Guard Company L from Watsonville had been sent to Nogales, Arizona, to help guard the U.S. border with Mexico against raids by Pancho Villa. When the contingent was disbanded and returned home to Watsonville, many faced mobilization again as more American soldiers were needed for World War I.

By mid-1918, almost 1,000 local men had been called to service. Remaining citizens supported the cause through purchase of War Savings Stamps. At one large meeting and rally in the casino in Santa Cruz, over $64,000 was raised to help finance the war effort.

The excitement of mobilization turned somber, however, as local men were reported killed in action. The press was particularly affected by the death of Edward Lorenson who had been city editor of the *Evening Pajaronian.*

Fortunately, the war soon ended. With the announcement of the Armistice in 1918, throngs of people rushed into the streets to celebrate.

Santa Cruz County entered the 1920s mirroring, politically, the rest of the country. From 1920 to 1930, the county of Santa Cruz voted Republican in each partisan election. Presidential candidates Warren Harding (1920), Calvin Coolidge (1924), and Herbert Hoover (1928) all won their elections by two-to-one margins over their Democratic rivals, and popular Republican Senator Hiram Johnson won the 1928 election by a four-to-one margin in Santa Cruz

County!

The 1920s also brought Prohibition. The Woman's Christian Temperance Union (WCTU) had been organized in 1874 and was especially strong locally in communities like Boulder Creek where the organization had its own meeting hall. The local WCTU chapters had a record of public service, including being the first major contributor to the Watsonville Public Library movement in 1896. The American Anti-Saloon League had also been organized in 1883, and it employed many local individuals in its powerful battle against "Demon Rum."

These organizations both had strong support in Santa Cruz County, and Prohibition's repeal on December 5, 1933, met with little local fanfare. Another reason for the lack of public relief when Prohibition ended was that "bootleg" liquor was available throughout the county. There were said to have been numerous stills in the Santa Cruz Mountains, and the beach at Rio del Mar became notorious as boatloads of liquor were unloaded there for illicit statewide distribution.

During the waning years of Prohibition, the country had entered the throes of the Great Depression. This brought the first change in Santa Cruz County's voting trends in a decade. The Depression did not affect this area as severely as it did other regions, probably because of the county's rural nature, agricultural and fishing industries, and its relatively small population. However, the effects were significant enough to cause this traditionally Republican stronghold to support several key Democratic candidates in the 1932 election.

Another contributing factor to the change in the voting pattern was the social violence which occurred locally during this period. In 1930 one of the most violent anti-Filipino riots in California's history occurred in Watsonville. Numerous Filipinos had moved to the Pajaro Valley during the 1920s to work in agriculture. There was local resentment against this new immigrant group, and nativist sentiment ran high. With the Depression and its attendant job scarcity, Filipinos were subjected to increasing abuse.

In January 1930 riots broke out near Watsonville, and mobs attacked Filipinos outside the local Monterey Bay Filipino Club. Increasing violence from January 19 until January 23 resulted in the death of one Filipino worker and injuries to several others. By the time the violence subsided in Watsonville, it had extended to other California communities.

The Filipino commissioner in Washington, D.C., spoke to the House of Representatives in protest, and a National Humiliation Day was observed on February 2, 1930, in Manila.

As the Depression wore on, agricultural strikes occurred within the Watsonville-Salinas area in 1936 which heightened tensions among county residents. The Fruit and Vegetable Worker's Union filed a complaint with the National Labor Relations Board alleging

Below: Pacific Avenue is shown here in 1927. Courtesy, the Sempervirens Fund

PRIDE, PREJUDICE, AND PROTEST

that the Grower Shipper Association of Watsonville-Salinas District refused to bargain collectively, and had practiced unfair labor tactics by blacklisting union workers.

While the Depression and its associated social unrest spelled gains for the Democratic Party in Santa Cruz County, the real solidifying factor was the beneficial effects of many of Franklin Delano Roosevelt's recovery programs. Civilian Conservation Corps (CCC) camps were established and their members performed work which otherwise would have been left undone. The camp at Big Basin Redwoods State Park left accomplishments still visible today, and the Pinto Lake Camp near Watsonville was so locally popular that details of its projects were common news items.

Besides the CCC, other recovery agencies were involved in assisting the area. The Works Progress Administration combatted soil erosion and performed other public works projects. The Public Works Administration funded Watsonville's high school gymnasium, and the Agricultural Adjustment Administration assisted the area's farmers through a plan of production control that successfully and profitably stimulated markets. The net effect of these programs increased business activity.

However, it was the increased activity generated by World War II that fully restored the county's economy. Throughout California the wartime expansion of 1942 and 1943 not only ended the Depression, but was responsible for one of the largest building booms in the state's history. And Santa Cruz County profited along with the rest of the state.

War necessitated increased military installations. Camp McQuaide, originally a National Guard encampment near the Capitola Airport, had been established in 1938. As a sub-post of Fort Ord in Monterey County, McQuaide was used to train units of the Coast Artillery and Signal Corps and had a 5,000-man training capacity. It was also used to house prisoners of war until it was closed in 1947.

Watsonville Airport was utilized as a Naval Auxiliary Air Station for bombers and fighter planes. The navy, as well as the Civil Aeronautics Authority, invested hundreds of thousands of dollars in the airport as it upgraded and expanded its facilities.

Also located near Watsonville was a Lighter than Air (LTA) auxiliary field. The blimps stationed there were used for antisubmarine patrol, although in one instance a blimp was dispatched from the Watsonville Naval Air Station to join the successful search for a navy fighter plane which had crashed in the Santa Cruz Mountains.

Volunteer efforts abounded as residents mobilized in Santa Cruz County to back the war effort. The Wilder Ranch on the north coast was an air-raid warning station staffed 24 hours a day by a local Scout troop. The Aptos Militia was organized as part of that community's civil defense measures. Victory gardens were planted

Above: As the county's population increased, the constable system in Santa Cruz County gave way to police departments. Santa Cruz Chief of Police William Walker who served from 1929-1931 illustrates the professional image which developed within the county's law enforcement agencies. Courtesy, UCSC Special Collections

SANTA CRUZ
CANNING CO
2808

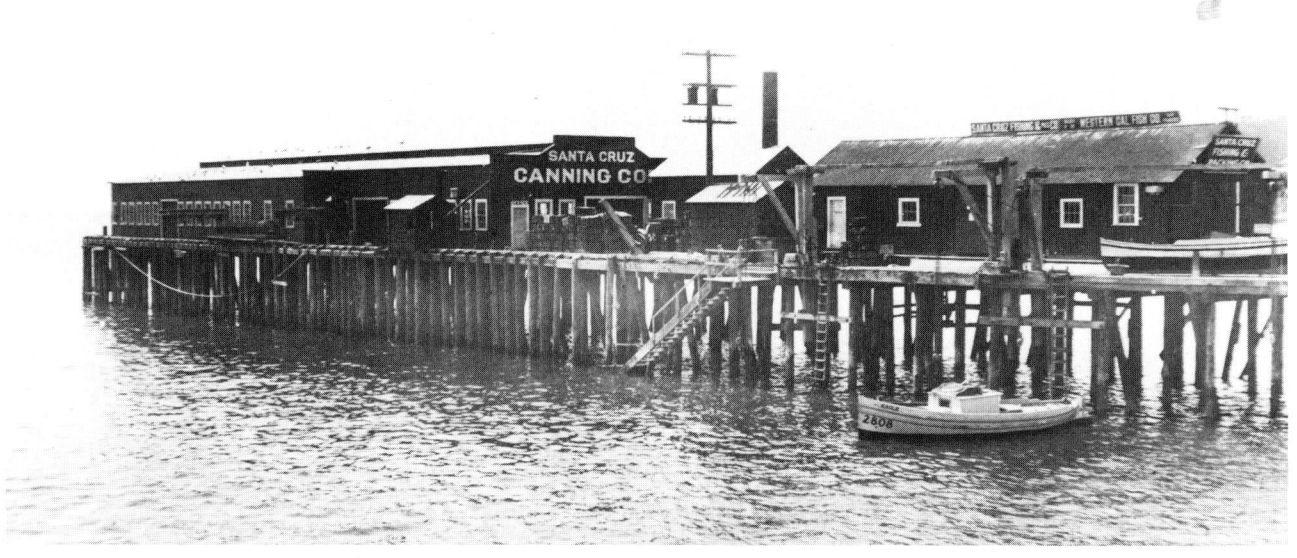

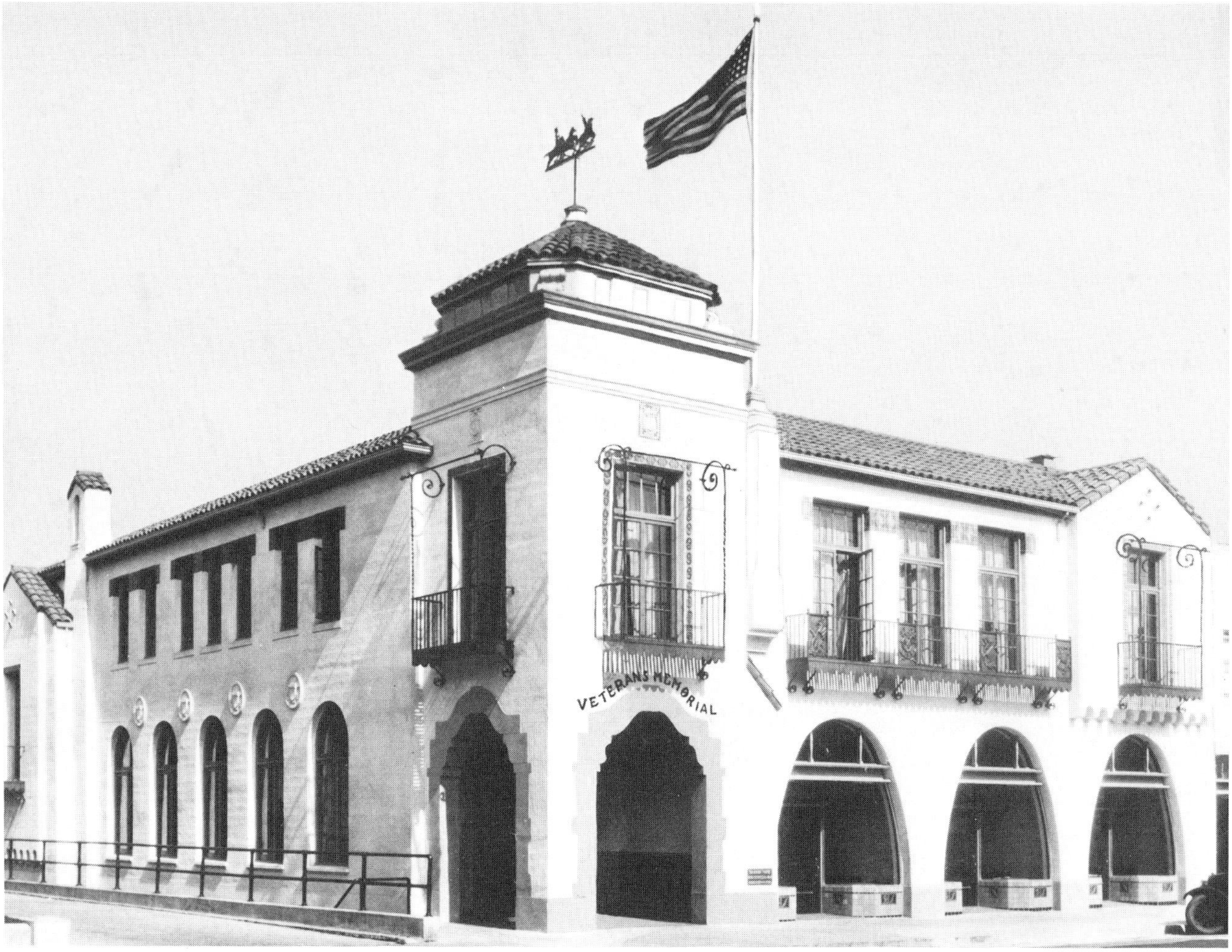
VETERANS MEMORIAL

PRIDE, PREJUDICE, AND PROTEST

throughout the county in an effort to conserve valuable commercial food production for the war effort, and numerous war stamps and bonds were purchased. Many individuals volunteered with the Red Cross, while others rushed to register as auxiliary firefighters and police officers. And men and women who had never been in an orchard before worked to save the Pajaro Valley apple crop.

One reason that farms in Santa Cruz County had to rely on volunteer labor was the "evacuation" of individuals of Japanese ancestry to relocation camps which began March 23, 1942. Many local Japanese had been engaged in agriculture and their removal created serious problems. But in spite of the demonstrated need for this labor force, anti-Japanese agitation was prominent in the county. And this agitation was not a new phenomenon. In the first decade of the twentieth century, the local press had called for stopping Japanese inroads into the "labor fields of this community." At the state level, in 1920 a measure extending the California Anti-Alien law to the Japanese passed by three to one! This law, which forbid aliens not eligible for citizenship to hold land titles, was a blatant anti-Japanese effort. When General John Dewitt of the Western Defense Command carried out orders barring enemy aliens from selected coastal zones and interring those of Japanese ancestry, it was welcomed locally as a necessary part of the war effort.

In addition to the devastating effects that the orders had on agriculture, the fishing industry on Monterey Bay was nearly crippled when Italian fishermen were barred from the coast as enemy aliens and Japanese fishermen were relocated. At the end of the war, many relocated Japanese moved back to the county where a new respect for their talents had been fostered by their absence.

Due to its proximity to the coast and therefore to the war effort, Santa Cruz County developed air raid, blackout, and defense procedures. These were not frivolous measures, as in late December of 1941, a Japanese submarine surfaced off the Santa Cruz coastline and began to shell a Richfield Oil Company tanker. The tanker safely reached Santa Cruz, and local residents performed their civil defense procedures with even more vigor!

When James Rickel, Jr., was killed aboard the USS *Yorktown*, he became the first Watsonville man to die in action. A year later, stores closed throughout Santa Cruz as an honor roll—inscribed with the 2,500 names of those from the area who were fighting—was dedicated. The war had become a stark reality for Santa Cruz County.

Following the war, local construction increased, retailers prospered, the area's economy grew, and Santa Cruz County once again embraced the Republican Party. Earl Warren handily won the area's support in his bid for governor, and other Republicans were returned to local offices. Beyond reestablishing its reputation as one of California's Republican enclaves, Santa Cruz County entered the postwar era with attention again focused on its tourist resources.

The Santa Cruz municipal wharf is shown here as it appeared in 1950. Courtesy, UCSC Special Collections

Although now out of fashion, memorial buildings were once common in communities throughout the United States. The Veteran's Memorial Building in Santa Cruz was constructed in 1931 as a monument to those from the area who had fought in previous wars. Courtesy, UCSC Special Collections

SANTA CRUZ COUNTY

This early 1900s "Welcome" on the southern city limits of the Santa Cruz-Los Gatos Highway expressed a sentiment that was true then and remains true today. Something is always going on in this restless paradise, and the welcome mat is out. Courtesy, UCSC Special Collections

Chapter Six

PARADISE REVISITED

In addition to focusing renewed attention on the tourist industry, the post-World War II boom period also generated an influx of permanent settlers to the county. In some instances, military personnel who had been stationed at Camp McQuaide or at nearby Fort Ord in Monterey County recognized the opportunities and advantages that resettling their families to California's Central Coast could provide. By 1950 the population of Santa Cruz County had grown to 66,534, which was almost double its 1930 population. The city of Santa Cruz reached 21,970 by the middle of this century. Ninety percent of the increase from 1940 to 1950 could be attributed to in-migration from other counties or states.

To accommodate this increased populace, the county was able to provide additional employment opportunities through "diversification of industry and the expansion of trade and service industries." A 1953 report prepared for the Santa Cruz Chamber of Commerce entitled "The Industrial Future of Santa Cruz" extolled the area's industrial potential and its optimum living conditions. But it also contained a statement which would prove to be all too prophetic: "... flood control along the San Lorenzo River is also an important problem on which future work will be needed." Two years later, on

Christmas Eve 1955, one-third of the city of Santa Cruz would lie under floodwaters of the San Lorenzo.

December 1955 had been a very wet month for the county. In the three-day period just before Christmas, rainfall of almost nine inches had been recorded in the city and up to 18 inches in the Santa Cruz Mountains. The resulting flood created a 22-foot-deep San Lorenzo River whose channel was double its normal width. To the south, flooding of Soquel Creek caused extensive damage in Soquel and Capitola. The mountain towns of Boulder Creek, Ben Lomond, Felton, and Zayante were all at least partially evacuated. In the Pajaro Valley, floodwaters threatened Freedom, Salsipuedes, Corralitos, and parts of Watsonville. Fortunately damage was less extensive in the south county even though the Pajaro River's flow exceeded the capacity of the levees which confined its lower reaches.

By the time floodwaters receded, eight lives had been lost, five of those in the city of Santa Cruz, and the county's property damage exceeded 10 million dollars. Water had been up to 14 feet deep in parts of Santa Cruz, and losses to businesses alone in that city amounted to four and a half million dollars. A sadly ironic note was that the potential for this kind of destruction had been recognized. A levee system to contain the San Lorenzo River through the city of Santa Cruz had been authorized by Congress, but funds had not yet been allocated.

Inasmuch as progress can come from disaster, the 1955 Flood provided the impetus and the basis for funding for the redevelopment of Santa Cruz. In 1956 the flood-damaged area received Federal Urban Renewal funds, and a Redevelopment District was established in Santa Cruz between Front, Soquel, Water, and Ocean streets. Levees were constructed by the Army Corps of Engineers and the San Lorenzo River and nearby Branciforte Creek were "contained." The controversy between the city and the county concerning which side of the river the new county administrative offices should be built on was eventually settled. And, by 1965, the west side of the San Lorenzo River sported the commercial development that the city had fought for. Unfortunately, several older historic structures such as the Garibaldi Hotel were razed, as engineers realigned streets and made room for modern buildings.

On the east side of the river, the County of Santa Cruz constructed its new $6-million Government Center. Dedicated in October 1967, the new facility had been discussed, planned, and postponed for over two decades. The five-story, 250,000-square-foot complex allowed county offices to be consolidated in one location, replacing the old 1895 courthouse, the Front Street Annex, and the numerous scattered offices that the county had been renting.

The face of Santa Cruz and of the county was changing, but not everyone agreed that the changes were beneficial, or even desirable. Controversy erupted over proposals for a new cross-town free-

Right: The Christmas Eve flood in 1955 sent a sea of water down Pacific Avenue in Santa Cruz. Merchants sandbagged to little avail. Property damage to businesses in the city alone exceeded $4 million. Courtesy, Covello & Covello Photographers

Below: As floodwaters receded, the extent of property damage from the 1955 disaster could be realized. Civil defense workers were aided by soldiers from Fort Ord in evacuating businesses and residences and caring for the displaced. Courtesy, Covello & Covello Photographers

way through, or at the edge of, Santa Cruz. Highway 1 had been widened from three lanes between Watsonville and Santa Cruz, and the next logical project seemed to be an easier connection between Highway 1 up the north coast and Highway 17 over the hill into the Santa Clara Valley. The freeway issue, along with several development proposals, served to involve and politicize the local citizens. In the case of the "Highways 4 and 100" issue, opponents to the proposals were successful.

Opponents were also successful at Lighthouse Field, where a planned complex containing hotel accommodations, convention facilities to serve over 1,000, and a marketplace with 100 shops, was thwarted. The original $13-million "Court of the Seven Seas" was planned in the early 1960s, but by 1967 seemed doomed due to lack of financing. In 1970 the Teachers Management and Investment Company purchased the land with the intent of building a convention center. The new project was to be a "New England Village" and would have included several 12-story buildings as well as "an authentic Atlantic coast community of 1860." Opponents claimed that it would also create a parking lot out of one-third of Lighthouse Field.

In mid-1972, the Save Lighthouse Point Association was formed to stop this development and permanently preserve the area as a public park. Eventually, after years of effort, this group was successful, and Lighthouse Field became part of the California State Park System.

Not all of the preservation in the county was spawned by controversy, though. In 1963 Chuck and Esther Abbott "retired" to Santa

Cruz and through low-key persistence changed the community as no one had since the days of Elihu Anthony and Frederick Hihn. The Abbotts, well-known photographers, were credited with being able to "see beauty that the rest of us could not." They perceived such beauty in the old Victorian buildings which were being rapidly razed in Santa Cruz to "make way for progress." The Abbotts purchased several older houses which were actually quite ordinary and proceeded to restore them. Their positive results inspired neighbors to refurbish their own homes, and the neighborhood acquired an upgraded image.

Nearby, a row of flats was badly in need of renovation. Chuck Abbott purchased them and, to facilitate their restoration, organized the Private Revitalization of Downtown. Using private money, PROD demonstrated the value of involving the community in its own revitalization. The group gained national attention as well as a grant from the federal Housing and Urban Development Department to share its model with other communities.

Chuck Abbott also saw potential beauty in Pacific Avenue. By the mid-1960s there were over 40 vacant stores on Santa Cruz's main street. Several of the major buildings had been "modernized" but something was obviously needed to stimulate this dying area. Abbott proposed that "the something needed" was a pedestrian mall. The Abbotts traveled thousands of miles photographing communities and building a case for the benefits, both esthetic and financial, of restoring a sense of atmosphere and charm to Pacific Avenue. Using color slide presentations, they convinced not only the community, but the merchants of Pacific Avenue, that salvation for the area lay in its

Far left: Built in 1887, this building housed C.D. Hinkle's mercantile business from 1894 until 1929. It subsequently became known as the McHugh and Bianchi building and was the center of controversy surrounding its demolition in the early 1970s. It was demolished in 1974. Courtesy, Covello & Covello Photographers

Left: By the 1960s, the bustle and activity that was evident on Pacific Avenue in this 1940s photo had drastically declined. Construction of the Pacific Garden pedestrian mall revitalized this area in the early 1970s. Courtesy, Covello & Covello Photographers

Below, left: The delicate balance between development and preservation that is necessary throughout the county is illustrated by the historic Bolcoff adobe on the coast south of Davenport. It was, at one point, to have become part of a subdivision development. It is now preserved as part of Wilder Ranch State Park. Courtesy, Monterey Bay Natural History Association

revitalization. So convincing were the Abbotts that more than two-thirds of the downtown property owners approved a plan to assess themselves for the cost of the project. The Pacific Garden Mall was started in 1969, and has proven to be an outstanding improvement for Santa Cruz, as well as a model of downtown revitalization.

Chuck Abbott was still not ready to retire, though. Realizing that after the construction of the new Government Center the old courthouse might well meet the fate of its predecessors, Abbott convinced Max Walden to purchase it. It was then preserved as the Cooper House, and since its restoration has served as a commercial complex.

For all of the successes the Abbotts had in Santa Cruz, they also suffered tragedy when their 18-year-old son Mark drowned in a surfing accident near Pleasure Point. In Mark's memory, Chuck and Esther Abbott had the lighthouse at Lighthouse Point rebuilt and donated to the city as a museum and park.

Chuck Abbott died on December 10, 1973, at the age of 80. But evidence of his vision and restless energy lives on in the city he affected so dramatically in his "retirement."

Another controversy erupted in 1971 which again pitted preservation against development. Golden West Savings of Oakland had purchased the McHugh and Bianchi building located at the hub of Pacific, Mission, and Water streets. The intention was to demolish the 90-year-old landmark to make room for a modern bank building. Opposition was voiced by local preservation and historical groups. The following year several thousand signatures were gathered on petitions to stop the demolition; and at about the same time, the building was placed on the National Register of Historic Places.

Ultimately all of this was to no avail. In 1974 the McHugh and Bianchi building was razed. But as a result of the interest and concern for preservation evident in the community, the Santa Cruz City Council created a Historic Preservation Commission that same year to identify and seek protection for significant historic structures.

Intensification of local interest in imminent development was not limited to the city of Santa Cruz during this period. In 1970, up the coast at Davenport, Pacific Gas and Electric Company secured an option to purchase 6,800 acres of Coast Dairies and Land property as the possible location for a nuclear power plant. Plans for the plant were eventually scrapped, but the proposal did serve to make county residents more aware of the north coast and of the need for a balanced plan of development and preservation, not only there but throughout the county.

By the late 1960s Santa Cruz County could boast many thousands of acres of public parklands. Stretching from county line to county line, were city, county, and state parks preserving natural beauty while allowing public access and enjoyment. For some, however, the Santa Cruz coast—and its waves—offer the most enjoyment.

Surfing may be a century-old activity in Santa Cruz. In the 1920s Hawaiian royalty graced the local waves and provided exciting demonstrations for beach-goers. The Santa Cruz Surfing Club was founded in 1936, and its dedicated members surfed on heavy, long, homemade boards. In the 1950s foam-and-fiberglass boards were introduced, and a local pioneer in the manufacture of surfing equipment, Jack O'Neill, first developed the wetsuit. Although wetsuits have proven invaluable to scuba divers, they also were extremely important to surfers who challenge the chilling Monterey Bay waters. By the 1960s Santa Cruz surfing spots like Pleasure Point, Steamer Lane, and Cowell Beach became dream destinations for surfers. The Beach Boys even mentioned Santa Cruz in their hit song "Surfin' USA." When the City of Santa Cruz opened the Surfing Museum in the Mark Abbott Memorial Lighthouse in May 1986, it became the first city to support such a facility. The establishment of the Surfing Museum seems to assure continued recognition of the significance of this sport in Santa Cruz.

The beaches along the bay have long been popular family vacation destinations as well. From 1927 until 1968, Southern Pacific brought people from San Francisco for a day on the beach aboard the "Suntan Special." The round-trip fare of three dollars enticed as many as 15,500 passengers a year to take the three-hour and 15-minute trip. The abandonment of this route by Southern Pacific didn't even make a dent in the number of visitors who make the trek over to the beach. Bumper-to-bumper traffic was, and still is, a summer weekend reality on Highway 17 between Santa Cruz and the Santa Clara Valley. To alleviate some of the traffic and parking pressures in beach areas, free shuttle bus service was set up in 1977 from outlying parking areas to Santa Cruz and Capitola area beaches. In one season, the beach shuttle carried 40,000 riders. At times it seemed, as a 1980 *Sunset* magazine article lamented, "Santa Cruz beach [was] . . . too popular."

Another beach attraction, the Boardwalk, which has served as a Santa Cruz landmark since the 1900s, was extensively renovated during the 1970s. The 1924 Giant Dipper, which is still rated as one of the top rollercoaster rides in the country, and the 1911 Carousel, which is said to be the oldest in continuous operation on the West Coast, were complemented by a restored Coconut Grove ballroom and casino. The Santa Cruz Boardwalk, one of the first beach amusement parks in the state, seems quite able to compete with the more modern amusement parks to the north and south.

The nearby Municipal Wharf, as well as the Esplanade in Capitola, and the city, county, and state beaches around them all serve to entice visitors from the more urban and hectic communities "over the hill" in the Santa Clara Valley and up the peninsula.

The county's attraction to tourists doesn't end at the water's

PARADISE REVISITED

Sempervirens Fund supporters gathered in Big Basin in 1975 to celebrate the seventy-fifth anniversary of the conservation movement in the Santa Cruz Mountains. Claude A. Look, a founder of the fund, is in the front with a bow tie. Dorothy Varian, whose efforts preserved Castle Rock State Park, is second from the right in the back row. Courtesy, Sempervirens Fund

This line of picnic tables at Seacliff State Beach near Aptos await the day's crowds which on summer weekends can number in the tens of thousands. Most of the county's coastline is accessible to the public. Courtesy, Monterey Bay Natural History Association

edge, however. Santa Cruz County is also known for its splendid mountain areas with their stands of exquisite redwoods. While logging has depleted much of this resource, pristine virgin forests are still quite evident along the ridge lines from Corralitos up into San Mateo County.

In Big Basin State Park, north of Boulder Creek, where California's State Park system began, the threat of development, so often a rallying point in modern county history, again fueled local interest and involvement. In 1968 a land developer proposed a subdivision on Mount McAbee which was outside park boundaries, but which would affect the watershed as well as requiring an entrance road through a park campground. The Sempervirens Club, which had worked originally to preserve the park, was by then almost defunct. The State of California was not in a position to purchase the developer's interest in the property although it did not support the development. And so, in the spirit that encompasses the regard and responsibility that Santa Cruz County's resources have long brought out in individuals, two men began a campaign to save Mount McAbee.

Claude A. "Tony" Look and Howard King took up the cause that Andrew Hill and the Sempervirens Club had championed. Christening their organization the Sempervirens Fund, Look and King succeeded in their efforts on Mount McAbee and established a conservation organization which has added thousands of acres to Big Basin. They also worked with Conservation Associates to establish Castle Rock State Park near Saratoga Summit. This park, which contains one of the premier climbing rocks in Central California, is a memorial to Russell Varian, a founder of Varian Electronics, whose dream it had been to preserve this area. After his death, his widow Dorothy Varian, along with Doris Leonard and George Collins, both established conservationists, founded Conservation Associates to achieve Varian's dream.

Working together, these two groups have not only protected two invaluable parks, but by using volunteer labor built a hiking trail from Saratoga Summit down through the two parks to the ocean at Waddell Beach. The Skyline-to-the-Sea Trail is a tribute to the concern and tenacity of caring conservationists who have worked relentlessly to help preserve this paradise.

Tourism and recreation are not the only important economic activities affecting modern Santa Cruz County. In the Pajaro Valley, agriculture and food processing retain their positions of premier importance. Labor disputes and threats by outside influences, ranging from encroaching air pollution from the neighboring Santa Clara Valley to treated sewage from Gilroy being introduced into the Pajaro River, often loom large. But the area and its people are well-rooted and well-served by their economic resources.

One of the most significant factors in modern Santa Cruz

SANTA CRUZ COUNTY

Left: Crown is one of the individual colleges that make up UCSC. Developed around the Oxford model, each college offers specialty areas of study. Campus growth necessitated a centrally located library and athletic, classroom, and laboratory facilities which are shared by the colleges. Courtesy, UCSC Photo Lab

Below, left: In fall 1968, then-Governor Ronald Reagan attended a Board of Regents meeting at UCSC. Student demonstrations centering on several issues, including the UFW Grape Boycott, met the Regents. During the demonstrations, Reagan and the Regents remained cloistered at Crown College. Courtesy, Covello & Covello Photographers

PARADISE REVISITED

County history may turn out to be the placement of the University of California campus here in 1965. In the following two decades, local population doubled, and much of this growth could be attributed to the university. A 1986 university master plan called for continued development and growth of the campus, projecting that by the year 2000, over 20 percent of the population of the city of Santa Cruz would be UCSC students.

But population increase and the development of the campus were never the only issues in the town/gown relationship. The establishment of the campus changed Santa Cruz into a university town. The initial friction between students and the often more conservative local businesspeople escalated during the late 1960s and 1970s when long hair and "hippie" clothing became *de rigueur* for most students, and when strike activities and demonstrations came down to town from the campus. At one time, some proponents of the cross-town freeway cited as a primary benefit the physical separation of the campus from the business district that would occur with the construction.

But the university remains, and the community of Santa Cruz as well as the rest of the county has learned to live with it, and to see it as a positive force. The university is a major employer as well as a supplier of student laborers for the local work force. And it has colored the community intellectually and supported it financially. Students seeking an understanding of themselves and of their place in the world have added to the restlessness of a community which is constantly striving to preserve and protect its surroundings and still make a living.

It has been said that Santa Cruz is a "state of mind." Citizens of this county are indeed unique and quite special. From the strawberry farmer of the Pajaro Valley, to the street mime in Santa Cruz, to the lumber mill owner on the north coast, there is a pervading sense of the splendor and wonder that make up this paradise called "Santa Cruz." There is also a restlessness. It seems partly a desire to achieve one's personal best to measure up to the surrounding natural best. There is an acknowledged need to protect the area's local beauty from those who would abuse or destroy it. And at the same time there is a willingness to share it. There is also a recognition that it is too fragile not to maintain a constant vigilance.

From Spanish explorers who upon seeing the area declared that it would be ideal for habitation to modern visitors seeking recreation and relaxation, Santa Cruz County has been seen as a paradise. From its earliest settlers who were not satisfied with mere existence but who sought a better life to its current citizens who struggle to preserve its qualities and feed its people, the easy way has seldom been taken.

Restless Paradise—it is a contradiction that has succeeded in Santa Cruz County.

Below: Demonstrations like this one—in honor of State School Superintendent Max Rafferty in 1968—escalated the following year as student and staff attention turned to the Vietnam War. Courtesy, Covello & Covello Photographers

SANTA CRUZ COUNTY

During the World War I era, the face of downtown Santa Cruz took on a "modern" look with paved streets, electricity, and the automobile. This crowd gathered around parading politicians on Pacific Avenue where it meets Soquel Avenue. Courtesy, UCSC Special Collections

Chapter Seven

PARTNERS IN PROGRESS

In 1943 mining engineer Henry G. Hubbard, while writing on the mines and mineral resources of the area, coined the phrase "Santa Cruz County, floral gem by sapphire sea." Perhaps this phrase, more so than any other, best defines that elusive spirit that has brought so many people to Santa Cruz County.

With the exception of the city and county of San Francisco, Santa Cruz is the smallest county in California. Yet it is also the most geographically diverse. To the northeast is the Santa Cruz Mountain Range, which acts as both a political and geographic boundary between Santa Cruz County and its neighboring counties. To the southwest is the Monterey Bay and Pacific Ocean coastline, which varies in topography from rugged, vertical sandstone cliffs, to rocky tidepools, to sandy beaches.

The county's natural resources have always been the guiding force behind Santa Cruz' commerce and industry. In the early 1890s, when settlers arrived in this Alta California area, they discovered the rich alluvial soils and mild climates of the Pajaro Valley and the bay and ocean coastline. Soon local agricultural pursuits flourished. Eventually the strawberry and apple of Watsonville, the brussels sprout of Davenport, the loganberry of Ben Lomond, and the cherry, plum, apricot, and wine grape of the Soquel and Glenwood areas became nationally known.

In time pioneers wandered into the mountains and discovered the rich forest and mineral wealth at hand. In 1841 Isaac Graham built the first water-powered sawmill in California at the junction of Bean and Zayante creeks. Twelve years later John Hines discovered significant quantities of gold in the coastal Ben Lomond Mountains. In 1857 a limestone business called Davis & Jordan got its start on the hill behind the city of Santa Cruz.

Because of Santa Cruz County's intrinsic beauty and its close proximity to the burgeoning San Francisco Bay Area, it was a natural for tourism. The many railroads, built deep into the mountains and along the coast to tap the previously mentioned wealth, provided access to remote areas. The many early hotels and retreats became immediate successes, and today tourism continues to thrive.

The Santa Cruz County businesses profiled in the following chapter have chosen to support both this publication and those continuing civic goals that make this floral gem by sapphire sea such a Restless Paradise.

SANTA CRUZ AREA CHAMBER OF COMMERCE

ABOVE: The Native Sons & Daughters of the Golden West were responsible for this 1888 Admissions Day parade down Pacific Avenue. Before the next parade the Santa Cruz Board of Trade came into being.

RIGHT: The Santa Cruz Chamber of Commerce started in the Bank of Santa Cruz building, and so it is appropriate that today it resides in the County Bank building.

Unlike many other California chambers, the Santa Cruz Area Chamber of Commerce has an impossible task at best. How do you balance the quality of life of the area at the same time you look after its economic future? How do you cooperatively work with other county, state, and national chambers while looking after the diverse interests of your own members? How do you become a catalyst between local governments, businesses, organizations, and individuals where farming, tourism, logging, quarrying, ranching, manufacturing, religious retreats, state and private recreational areas, commercial industries, wholesale and retail outlets, health care providers, educational institutions, and environmental preservation groups represent the various interests of your membership? Welcome to the everyday headaches with which the Santa Cruz Area Chamber of Commerce has to deal. But deal it does, and quite well, ever since the organization got its start as the Board of Trade back in 1889.

It all began 98 years ago, when the Board of Trade was organized to "educate people from other parts of the country on the merits of locating in Santa Cruz." At that time the area was a prime California manufacturer/supplier of many of the construction materials and foodstuffs so necessary for the hungering westward expansion. Because of the efforts of the early Board of Trade many onetime visitors would remain as residents.

As the westward expansion gradually slowed and everyday life in California began to settle down, the goals and objectives of the Santa Cruz area started to change. On January 6, 1909, the Board of Trade gave way to the new Santa Cruz Chamber of Commerce, whose "main thrust was to promote community pride, beautification, cleanliness, and civic improvement." In conjunction with this, the primary local goal became promoting year-round tourism.

The 1987 Santa Cruz Area Chamber of Commerce has grown from its original 254 members to well over 1,000. Because of this the chamber, while continuing to support its original goals, has grown with the community to include many more objectives. Today, according to executive director Lionel Stoloff, "we spend a great deal of time on economic development. We have been directly responsible for bringing Wrigley's, Lipton, AT&T, Synertek, the University of California, and the Yacht Harbor here. We are working to strike a balance between the expansion plans of the University of California, Santa Cruz, and the impact on city housing, water, and sewer capabilities."

Another new objective is the chamber's Leadership Santa Cruz program where it is helping to build future leaders. The program takes 30 individuals from the community and puts them through nine months of training in leadership skills, communication skills, and familiarizes them with each sector of the community. Out of 600 chambers, the Santa Cruz Area Chamber of Commerce is one of only 18 in California providing such a program.

When all is said and done the chamber also does those day-to-day things that make it such a valuable community resource. On the average the Santa Cruz Area Chamber of Commerce answers 50 letters of inquiry and 180 phone calls per day. As to the future, Stoloff says, "Santa Cruz will be a continuing, viable marketplace, but growth and development will not be at the expense of our quality of life."

HARRY H. FUKUTOME NURSERY

One of the true floral gems of Santa Cruz County is the Harry H. Fukutome Nursery on Freedom Boulevard in Watsonville. There, in several wooden and steel-frame, fiberglass-roofed, air-conditioned greenhouses, can be found row after row of every type and color of flowering carnation imaginable. Among these are the traditional reds, pinks, whites, and tangerines, as well as the stylish paris, silver-pinks, ace, and exquisites. In all, more than 183,000 square feet is devoted to the tender care and cultivation of 200,000 continuously producing plants.

However, the story of the Fukutome Nursery goes far beyond just the current facts and figures at hand. For it is also a part of the larger history of what has become the number one greenhouse and cut-flower-growing area in the United States today.

The story began back around 1955, when Henry Sakae started growing carnations in a small greenhouse nursery in Soquel. Achieving moderate success, it wasn't long before he wanted to expand his enterprise. Drawn by the perfect flower-growing climate of the Pajaro Valley area, he sold out his Soquel facility in 1958 and moved to his present location in Watsonville. It was about that time that Ben Graust opened a greenhouse nursery on Freedom Boulevard and became one of the two cut-flower growers in the Pajaro Valley. In 1962 they were followed by Arne Thirup and Mits Nakashima.

The same year three young Japanese laborers, working in a San Francisco Bay Area carnation nursery, became interested in an old Watsonville apple orchard on Condit Lane that was for sale. Long on intestinal fortitude and short on capital, Akira and Osamu Nagamine and their brother-in-law, Harry Fukutome, pooled their resources and bought the five-acre property. With lots of hard work and some educational help from the U.C. Agricultural Extension Service the Nagamine and Fukutome Nursery soon came into being.

By 1966 the nursery had prospered to such an extent that the three partners decided to each go into business for themselves. Thus, Osamu Nagamine took over the Condit Lane nursery, and Akira Nagamine and Harry Fukutome bought and equally divided a 25-acre apple orchard on Freedom Boulevard. In 1967 the three nurseries became separate entities, which to this day still continue at the same locations.

From these early beginnings has come the Monterey Bay Flower Growers Association, comprised of 130 members who devote more than 26 million square feet of continuous growing space in the Salinas and Pajaro valleys to the cultivation of carnations, orchids, chrysanthemums, roses, and various potted plants.

Like many association members, Harry H. Fukutome has come a long way since he began his business. Perhaps one of his more meaningful achievements

Members of the founding families pose in October 1962 shortly after the opening of the Nagamine-Fukutome Nursery. In the back row (left to right): Harry Fukutome, Mrs. Osamu (Daisy) Nagamine, Mrs. Arika (Hideko) Nagamine, Mrs. Harry (Teruko) Fukutome, Osamu Nagamine, and in the front row (left to right) Irene Fukutome, Glen Nagamine, Roy Nagamine, Akira Nagamine (kneeling), Janet Nagamine, Doris Nagamine, and James Nagamine.

was his selection as Farmer of the Year by the Santa Cruz Farm Bureau in 1986.

Today, with the help of Harry's wife, Teruko, his daughter, Irene, and 12 full-time employees, the Harry H. Fukutome Nursery produces about 4 million carnation blooms per year. This translates to more than 5,000 boxes of 700-count flowers. Of these, about 20 percent go to local California customers, while about 4,000 boxes find their way to clients in Ohio, Washington, Idaho, Connecticut, New York, and Hawaii.

SANTA CRUZ SEASIDE COMPANY BOARDWALK

In this 1890s view, taken from the wharf, the pre-Fred Swanton, Santa Cruz Seaside Company beach/boardwalk area is seen.

If you were to walk up to a total stranger on any street, anywhere in California, and ask them if they knew where the city of Santa Cruz was located, chances are they would respond, "Isn't that where the Boardwalk is?" The Santa Cruz Boardwalk, the oldest and only beachside amusement park left on the West Coast, is alive and well after 80 years of continuous operation by the Santa Cruz Seaside Company. Not only is the Boardwalk a place where more than 2 million people annually come to enjoy its many traditional attractions, but also, because of its longevity, it has become a place of historical significance.

It is hard to say when the history of the Boardwalk began. It could have been clear back in 1857, when Elihu Anthony built the first wharf out into Monterey Bay. Soon coastal ships were tying up at Port Santa Cruz, and the beach/boardwalk area was fast becoming a well-known place to visit. Perhaps it was in 1875, when passengers aboard the early Santa Cruz Railroad trains first admired the beauty of the gentle sea and surf, the white sandy beaches, and the expanding boardwalk that lined it all. Or maybe it was in the 1880s, when the narrow gauge South Pacific Coast trains brought thousands of tourists from San Francisco, Alameda, and other Bay Area cities and towns. By then coastal hotels abounded, bathing baths and swimming were pleasant pastimes, and there was always the beach itself.

It was Fred Swanton who put his dream of turning the Santa Cruz beach and boardwalk area into a West Coast Coney Island into action in 1903. With the acquisition of two local bathhouses, the construction of several cottages and a tent city, and the completion of a family casino and a pleasure pier, his dream was deemed a great success within one year.

Unfortunately, he suffered a disastrous fire in 1906, and much of his effort was lost. Undaunted, he rebounded and rebuilt. He began by bringing in famed architect William H. Weeks, who laid out plans for a new ballroom, to be known as the Cocoanut Grove; an indoor swimming pool, later called "the Plunge"; another pleasure pier; and a boardwalk. In 1908 Swanton added a thrill ride, the L.A. Thompson Scenic Railway, a gentle roller coaster. Two years later the $500,000 Casa Del Ray Hotel went up. In 1911 Swanton's final vision for his Coney Island West occurred when world-renowned Danish woodcarver, Charles I.D. Looff, delivered a brand-new carousel, complete with hand-carved wooden horses.

Fred Swanton's Casino, Plunge, and Cocoanut Grove are seen in this rare night photo taken from the pleasure pier shortly after it opened in 1907.

As with all great enterprises, the chance for failure looms large. By 1912 Swanton had spread himself so thin he found himself having to declare bankruptcy. Soon local investors organized the Santa Cruz Seaside Company to acquire the many Swanton Boardwalk-related enterprises. From that day to this the firm has owned and operated the Boardwalk and the nearby Casa Del Ray Hotel, now a retirement hotel.

To talk about the history of the Boardwalk is to talk about its many attractions such as the Cocoanut Grove, the Giant Dipper roller coaster, and the carousel.

Although the current Cocoanut Grove is a modern, multiuse facility, complete with 6,000-square-foot glass-ceilinged convention-banquet room and corporate meeting and conference rooms, a short walk into its ballroom is like stepping back in time. Crystal chandeliers, gold leaf, and elegant draperies blended with Victorian decor set the historic mood where ghosts of the elegant past abound. Over the years the ballroom has played host to such legends as Artie Shaw, Benny Goodman, Les Brown, Lionel Hampton, and Count Basie. To this day the Cocoanut Grove is routinely visited by entertainment greats, from rock stars to the big bands of yesterday and today.

Another Boardwalk favorite is the 76-year-old carousel. No longer just an amusement ride, it is now a historical artifact. Each of the 70 Looff-carved horses would today bring an average of $8,000 each. Famous for their long, flowing manes, jewel-studded bridles, muscular legs, and spirited expressions, they are working antiques created by a handcrafted skill that has been lost to history. In addition, the carousel's classic 1894, 342-pipe, German-made Ruth band organ is one of the last of its kind in the world. The Santa Cruz Seaside Company takes great pride in keeping this carousel operating and in original condition.

While the carousel is the oldest of the 75 Boardwalk rides and attractions, the all-wood Giant Dipper, built in 1924 to replace the original L.A. Thompson Scenic Railway, is the "King." Recognized as one of the 10 best roller coasters in the world, its zero-to-55-mile-per-hour initial 70-foot drop has been experienced by more than 27 million riders. Recently both the carousel and the Giant Dipper were declared National Historic Landmarks by the U.S. Park Service.

Of course, the Cocoanut Grove, the carousel, and the Giant Dipper are just three of the many Boardwalk attractions. In addition, there are the other rides, restaurants, gift shops, concessions, games, and the beach itself. There also are an-

The Giant Dipper is surrounded on three sides by water (the San Lorenzo River and Monterey Bay). It has been in this position for the past 63 years, maintained but unchanged.

nual events such as the Clam Chowder Cookoff, the Brussels Sprout Festival, the Budweiser Tug-of-War competition, and the Christmas Craft Festival. Approximately 1,100 seasonal employees are required to support these attractions and activities.

In recent years the fame of the Boardwalk has even spread to Hollywood. Movies such as Clint Eastwood's thriller *Sudden Impact, Sting II* with Jackie Gleason, and the 1987 Warner Brothers comic-horror film *Lost Boys* have all helped to keep the Santa Cruz Seaside Company Boardwalk in the public eye.

Since admission is free, the Boardwalk remains the best value for traditional amusement park entertainment anywhere on the West Coast. Under the continuing leadership of Charles Canfield, president; Robert Millslagle, vice-president; and Edward Hutton, general manager, the Santa Cruz Seaside Company Boardwalk will no doubt continue to build on a long history that has already made it a quality Partner in Progress in Santa Cruz County.

The 1987 Santa Cruz Seaside Company Boardwalk has 22 major rides, including the Jet Star and Loggers Revenge.

WATSONVILLE NURSERIES

Nestled in the foothills of the Santa Cruz Mountains, just east of the city of Watsonville, is an area of the Pajara Valley known as the banana belt. It is so named because the temperature almost never drops below freezing and because it offers perfect climatic conditions for the growing of flowers and fragile vegetables and fruits. Taking advantage of this situation is one of California's prime rose growers, the DiCicco family, and their Watsonville Nurseries. There more than 350,000 quality hybrid-tea and miniature bare-root rose plants are continuously being grown in 85 peaks, or greenhouses, on about 600,000 square feet of dedicated land. Collectively, these plants annually produce from 12 to 15 million saleable cut flower blooms for the Watsonville Nurseries.

In order to properly market their roses, the DiCicco family has Watsonville Nurseries divided into two separate organizations. The first is the growing concern that provides, cuts, places in water, grades, and sells the roses. The second is the shipping organization that buys the roses, contacts and contracts the wholesalers and retailers, and ships the boxed flowers, under the "Sunnyvale" label, nationwide via truck and/or airplane.

The Sunnyvale tie to Watsonville has to do with the history of the label itself. Back in 1946 Jules DiCicco and his wife, Florance, opened a flower shop in San Mateo that they successfully operated for the next six years. In January 1952 they were presented with the opportunity to buy a well-known 175,000-square-foot greenhouse nursery in Sunnyvale that had been in operation since 1929. They jumped at the chance, and thus began the DiCicco family cut-flower nursery business. For the next 12 years their business grew and prospered.

In 1964 the couple's son Gene entered the family business, the rose operation was expanded to 250,000 square feet of greenhouses, and the Sunnyvale sales label was adopted. Before long the label was recognized nationwide as representing both quality and integrity in the rose business.

Unfortunately for the DiCiccos, just about the time things began going well for the nursery, the City of Sunnyvale started into a growth and development spiral that would literally force the family out of the area by 1972. Thus, as early as 1965 they were looking elsewhere to expand. In short order the DiCiccos found and purchased the current Watsonville property. In 1967 they began building their new greenhouses, and soon Watsonville Nurseries became a reality. In 1970 the couple's second son, Douglas, joined the organization.

Today the family-run business, now in its third generation, finds Gene DiCicco overseeing the entire operation and its 45 full-time employees. Helping him is his daughter, Kelly Siefke, who works in the office, and his son, Bob, who is in charge of greenhouse maintenance and construction. In addition, Douglas' son Kirk is production manager and his other son, Jefferey, is sales manager. Florance DiCicco became president of Watsonville Nurseries fullowing the death of her husband in 1986.

As to the future, Gene DiCicco says, "We currently have more longtime steady customers than flowers. Although the foreign growers have about 30 percent of the U.S. rose market, they can't compete with us quality-wise, and that's what makes the difference. Also, the fact that Congress recently made the rose the national flower of the United States won't hurt."

WYCKOFF, RICHARDSON, SANSON, ALLEN AND LOCKE-PADDON

Unlike most histories that follow a time line or describe an expanding series of events, the history of a law firm is a rather static process. Because it is a one-to-one business between lawyer and client, its future is not generally based on its past. To quote Bruce Richardson, current senior partner of Wyckoff, Richardson, Sanson, Allen and Locke-Paddon, "When you freeze frame it, a law firm is just the people that are there at the time they are there." For the Wyckoff law firm, which has been successfully providing the Monterey Bay area with full legal services for the past 88 years, this is especially true.

The history of the firm traces back to 1899. A young, energetic Hubert Coke Wyckoff, after completing six years of college and passing the California State Bar, had returned home to go into partnership with practicing attorney William L. Rodgers. The partnership was short lived, however, as by 1900 Rodgers had moved on. Wyckoff next found himself practicing with famous lawyer, orator, and former county district attorney, Julius Lee. In 1901 another young attorney, John E. Gardner, joined the firm of Lee & Wyckoff. Almost immediately the two young lawyers hit it off. Under Lee's tutelage the relatively inexperienced Wyckoff and Gardner soon learned the difference between the textbook law they had studied and the 30 years of practical local experience garnered by their senior partner.

In January 1903 Wyckoff and Gardner took over the practice from the now Judge Lee, and the law firm of Wyckoff & Gardner came into being. For the next 18 years the partners would provide every kind of imaginable legal service necessary for an up-and-coming farming community such as Watsonville—John Gardner as a widely respected trial lawyer, and Hubert Coke Wyckoff as a valued counselor.

From that day to this, although practicing in various locations in Watsonville, the firm has remained locally based. Included in the list of former

An advertisement for the early law firm from the Watsonville Pajaronian, *May 18, 1899.*

partners are Harry M. Parker, James A. Wyckoff, Hubert C. Wyckoff, Jr., Philip T. Boyle, Willard Lee Pope, Harry F. Brauer, and Richard W. Kessell.

Although the day-to-day, client-by-client stories of the various partners cannot be told, some hints of their abilities and successes remain. Among other things, Hubert Coke Wyckoff served as president of the California State Bar in 1921 and 1931. Harry M. Parker and James A. Wyckoff served on the board of governors of the state bar, with Parker a vice-president in 1951 and Wyckoff vice-president and treasurer in 1963. Hubert C. Wyckoff, Jr., was a leading arbitrator of industrial disputes throughout the United States. Harry F. Brauer is now a justice of the California Court of Appeals, and Richard W. Kessell is now a municipal court judge in Santa Cruz.

Today the six members of the firm—Bruce Richardson; Ralph Sanson, a former chairman of the Santa Cruz County Board of Supervisors; Richard Allen; William Locke-Paddon; Stephen Weldon; and Robert Johnson—continue the "first-floor operation." Richardson equates law firm charges to the height of law buildings in San Francisco. "You should have hourly rates posted at each floor because I know they increase the higher up you get in the building." However, being an attorney in Watsonville is an entirely different matter. Says Richardson, "We have to serve a broad base of clients face to face. Unlike a multimillion-dollar corporation where the legal fees are just a bill in a pile of bills, the dentist next door has to figure out how many teeth to fill in order to pay our bill." As to where lawyers stand in the great Watsonville scheme of things, Richardson relates: "I had a woman come in one day and she had to see me right away, without an appointment. The reason was that she didn't want to be late for her beautician. I saw her immediately."

KITAYAMA BROTHERS

To talk about the Santa Cruz County flower industry is to talk about Kitayama Brothers, the largest grower and individual shipper of flowers in the United States. Their current joint operations comprise three distinct corporations and three operations.

Kitayama Brothers, the growing corporation, involves three different growing locations. The first is in Union City, where Tom and Ted Kitayama look after 35 acres of greenhouses and a western wholesale floral marketing/shipping organization known as Golden State Wholesale Florist. The second location is in Watsonville, where Kee Kitayama is responsible for one million square feet of greenhouses and 175 acres of outside growing land. The third facility, originally started by Ray Kitayama and now run by a nonfamily manager, is

Roses carefully being prepared for boxing prior to shipment at the Watsonville Kitayama Brothers facility.

in Brighton, Colorado. The Brighton manager oversees the growing operation and 15 midwestern and western outlets of Green Leaf wholesale florists.

The second Kitayama corporation, headquartered in Watsonville, is U.S. Flowers. Organized in 1983 to be much like Green Leaf, it is primarily the marketing arm of Kitayama Brothers' Watsonville operation. U.S. Flowers provides brokerage and shipping for Kitayama Brothers flowers and those of many other local growers to points all over the United States. In addition to Watsonville, U.S. Flowers also has outlets in Fresno and the Los Angeles Flower Market.

To say that the Kitayama brothers have come a long way is an understatement. They had to overcome both the normal adversities of an expanding business and those of historical prejudice. The four brothers grew up on Bainbridge Island, Washington, where their Japanese parents worked a small rented greenhouse. It was rented because an alien land law in Washington forbade them land ownership. With the beginning of World War II most of the family was uprooted and forced to live in concentration camps, first in California and later in Idaho. Fortunately the oldest brother, Tom, who was studying horticulture at Washington State, was allowed to graduate.

In 1948 the four brothers received their first real break in business. Tom was working for a nursery in San Leandro, while brothers Ted and Ray were at a greenhouse grower in Mt. Eden. As soon as brother Kee graduated from Ohio State the four were able to buy a 16-acre site in Alvarado, now Union City. There they started Kitayama Brothers and began building their own greenhouses.

Until the early 1950s the growing and distribution of flowers was very localized. As a result, markets were small. With the advent of air freight, however, the flower markets soon expanded nationwide. For the Kitayama Brothers this meant phenomenal potential for growth. From 1950 to 1966 Kitayama Brothers would go from a few greenhouses to more than 35 acres of greenhouses at two nearby locations. Green Leaf was founded in 1959 to handle the marketing and large shipping volume Kitayama Brothers was seeing.

As the Union City facility filled to capacity, the four brothers realized that it didn't take four managers to run the business, and that there was still plenty of room for expansion in the marketplace. In 1966 Ray moved to Colorado where he established the Brighton facility to pursue midwestern markets. In 1970 Kee moved on to Watsonville to establish the Kitayama Brothers Greenhouse

The Kitayama Brothers' Watsonville nursery has one million square feet of greenhouses and 175 acres of outside growing land.

overlooking Sunset Beach.

Choosing the Watsonville site was a long process for Kee Kitayama; he spent considerable time trying to find the perfect location. His search took him up and down the Pacific Coast, and he even considered Mexico and Columbia. Finally he settled on the Watsonville site because it offered the best climate and shipping conditions. Since the site was next to the ocean, both greenhouse plants and outside flowers could be grown in the good average temperature. The summer fog would reduce the sunlight reaching the greenhouses, and the mild winter temperatures would make it possible to grow outdoor flowers. While generally not very good for general agriculture, the 100-percent marine sand, with its porousness, was ideal for growing flowers. The abundance of local agriculture meant freight distribution was already well established.

Throughout its history Kitayama Brothers has faced moments of hardship. In 1978 the Brighton, Colorado, facility had been expanding, while all the time keeping its warehouses and boiler room, which heated the greenhouses, centrally located. One dark, cold, December night a fire started in the boiler room. In short order everything was in flames. Soon thereafter, with the boilers shut down, it didn't take long for the minus-14-degree outside temperature to kill most plants at the facility. And just a few months after the Colorado disaster the 22-greenhouse facility Kitayama Brothers had recently purchased from Union Carbide in Watsonville was set upon by a freak tornado off the ocean that severely damaged all but one of the greenhouses. Kee Kitayama relates, "My wife and I were about to leave on a trip to the Holy Lands, but we cancelled because my wife felt bad luck runs in threes." It would take almost seven years for Kitayama Brothers to financially recover from the two disasters.

Today Kitayama Brothers is on the rebound. The Watsonville facility currently produces about 17 million blooms from more than 40 varieties of roses per year. At the old Union Carbide greenhouses the organization grows miniature carnations, astromarias, smilax, lillies, and ferns. In addition, depending on the season, more than 5 million iris bulbs are grown outside, along with heather, agapanthus, three kinds of statis, daffodils, and gladiolas. It takes about 100 full-time, well-trained employees to accomplish the growing, handling, packaging, marketing, and shipping of Kitayama flowers, just at Watsonville.

Kitayama Brothers is currently constructing a new facility in Watsonville, known as the Park View Greenhouses. It will be a stand-alone operation with its own computer-automated environmental control systems, installed in the latest in glass greenhouse technology and incorporated with necessary handling and warehouse facilities. The only thing in common with the other Watsonville operations will be the marketing by U.S. Flowers. A new marketing organization is being established, Cal Pacific Flowers, to service the major supermarket chains in the West.

Although the business has changed significantly over the past 40 years Kitayama Brothers' original slogan still applies: "Quality, service, and a little bit more."

The four founders of Kitayama Brothers are from left (standing) Kee and Ted, and (in front, seated) are Tom, mother Masu (now deceased), and Ray.

Kee Kitayama—co-owner and supervisor of the Watsonville location of Kitayama Brothers—and his family, who all grew up in Santa Cruz County. From left are Joyce; Diane; Kee; Kee's wife, Keiko; Kathy; Kristine; and John.

RICHARD A. SHAW, INC., FROZEN FOODS

Imagine a frozen food facility that produces more than 100 million pounds of product per year, a process that involves 36 different vegetables, prepared 110 different ways, packaged under 250 separate U.S. frozen food company labels, and that employs 1,100 people during peak season to accomplish all this, and you have the current Shaw frozen food facility in Watsonville. Add to this a brokerage arm that can provide the consumer with 75 different fresh frozen fruits and vegetables, processed in 160 possible styles, and you have Richard A. Shaw, Inc., Frozen Foods, or more aptly put by its president Richard A. "Dick" Shaw, "one-stop shopping."

To discuss the history of Shaw Frozen Foods is to really look at three separate entities that are all intertwined: Richard Shaw, the frozen food industry itself, and a change in food preservation technology.

In 1933 Shaw started his career in food processing on Cannery Row in Monterey where he removed livers from Basking sharks, which were to be used in a recognized liquid health tonic of the time. From there he went to fish reduction, and eventually, in 1937, he became a foreman at one of the local canneries.

From Cannery Row Shaw took a turn in 1938 as a golf professional at Monterey Bay Golf and Country Club. That was followed by a job with Union Oil as a lubricating sales engineer during the construction of the Fort Ord military base. In 1944 Shaw did a stint in the Army at Camp Roberts where he was a technical instruction sergeant. With Shaw's background in food processing and fluid systems, getting into the frozen food business after the war was a natural, and once the U.S. economy turned peacetime, the industry was ready for him.

The freezing process had been around since the late 1920s, when pie-filling companies first started preserving fresh fillers so they would be available year round. In the 1930s the business expanded into vegetables. Although the technology was available during that period to produce large quantities of frozen foods, the industry never really got off the ground. This was because the average household, equipped only with an ice box, had no way to keep frozen foods for any length of time. During the war the military caused a considerable increase in bulk business, which was followed by a downturn in the postwar years. No less than 11 companies in Watsonville that had thrived on the war business went bankrupt after it was over.

In November 1945 Shaw went to work for Western Frozen Foods. By the summer of the following year he had worked himself up to superintendent. In 1947 he became the manager at Fresh Frozen Foods. Four years later Shaw joined Watsonville Canning & Frozen Foods to start up and oversee its entire freezing operation. He accepted the position and would stay with the company for the next 21 years. By the time Shaw left, Watsonville Canning & Frozen Foods had become a 100-million-pound-per-year producer.

It was during the late 1940s and early 1950s that refrigerators with freezing compartments began to replace the ice boxes in most American homes—a development that proved to be a phenomenal boom to the frozen food industry. As Shaw points out, "When I left Watsonville Canning & Frozen Foods in 1972, it only took me 10 minutes to process and

Richard A. Shaw, founder and president of Richard A. Shaw, Inc., Frozen Foods.

An aerial view of the Shaw Frozen Foods plant in Watsonville.

freeze what their annual total production had been in the previous year."

Possessed with the dream of operating his own company, Shaw spent the next four and one-half years generating the financing to begin Shaw Frozen Foods. His dream was a large one. He wanted to build a straight line plant, using the latest in frozen food technology, where seven different lines of product could operate at the same time and have a production capability of 250 million pounds per year. He wanted his plant to be the most modern and most productive facility in the world. In 1976 Shaw saw his dream become a reality. From that day to this, with the help of his wife, Joann; his four sons, Steve, Bruce, Dick, and Jeff; and daughter, Jennifer, he has made Shaw Frozen Foods a leader in the industry.

Watsonville proved to be an ideal location for a frozen food facility; it is the center of all the major growing areas in central and Northern California. Close at hand are the Pajaro and San Benito valleys, to the north is the Pacific Ocean coastline, to the east are the Santa Clara and San Joaquin valleys, and to the south is the Salinas Valley.

The Salinas Valley is the most productive vegetable-growing area in the world for its size. A constant temperature, coupled with other climatic conditions, offers growers a 12-month growing season. Shaw says that the quality of the vegetables grown there is such that "you would have to purposely destroy any Salinas Valley product to make it bad."

Because Watsonville is centrally located, vegetables cut in the fields can be processed within hours. Thus, the best vegetables grown anywhere on earth, coupled with the shortest processing times, makes Watsonville the frozen vegetable capital of the world.

Shaw Frozen Foods packages and freezes millions of pounds of quality vegetables year round. Broccoli, spinach, cauliflower, brussels sprouts, and asparagus are just a few of the products that are processed annually at Shaw's.

Today Shaw Frozen Foods continues to operate in a less-than-perfect market. Not only processors, but also growers, are seeing stiff competition from foreign sources. To that end Dick Shaw has founded a nonprofit corporation called THANKS (Together Helping Americans Nationwide Keep Strong). Its message, to which he has devoted much energy, is "Support our Farmers—Buy American."

As to the future of the frozen food business, Shaw states that since 1947 "the frozen food industry has gone from slightly under a half-million pounds to well over 7 billion pounds of product per year to the consumer." Ironically, another technological change is taking place in the kitchens of America, the microwave oven, which may bring a new boom to the frozen food industry. If such is the case, one thing is certain: Richard A. Shaw, Inc., Frozen Foods is ready to meet the challenge.

As a former member of the United Nations Committee, Richard Shaw has his employees raise the United Nations flag. He also founded a nonprofit corporation called THANKS (Together Helping Americans Nationwide Keep Strong) to which he has devoted much time and energy to support the American farmer.

MONTEREY MUSHROOMS

Premium medium and button mushrooms are seen in their familiar prepack and bulk containers shortly before shipment.

Often when creative entrepreneurs change businesses it can be quite dramatic. So it must have been for Dave and Roy Claassen when they went from controlling the fast-paced Shelby/Cobra automobile organization and selling high-performance auto parts, to the slow, methodical growing of mushrooms. Dramatic or not, in 1971, under the name of Monterey Mushrooms, the Claassen brothers leased a large chicken farm in the Prunedale area near Watsonville, converted a few chicken coops into processing rooms, and began the above-ground growing of mushrooms.

Initially the operation required few employees and was small in scope. In just four short years, however, because of the Claassens' engineering skills and increasing consumer demand, that all changed. By 1975 Monterey Mushrooms had grown to the position where 35 full-time employees were successfully producing more than 2 million pounds of mushrooms per year.

It was about this time that Amfac, a large agribusiness company, began to take a keen interest in the Claassen enterprise. Before long agreements were drawn up, which included the Claassens staying on to manage the operation, and Amfac became the new owner of Monterey Mushrooms. From 1975 to 1979 Monterey Mushrooms continued to grow at a phenomenal rate. Growth as far as plant size was concerned was easy as the company simply expanded into more and more chicken coops. Growth in terms of quantity and quality, however, required both management and technical resources.

As the physical plant expanded over sixfold, yield rate efficiencies increased 150 percent. Sophisticated growing technology, climate control equipment, research and development, and attention to the "art of mushroom growing" made this growth possible. As a result, by the end of the second four-year period Monterey Mushrooms was producing from 12 to 15 million pounds of mushrooms.

Having become regarded as a leader in the industry and community, Monterey Mushrooms was well positioned for further growth. For openers, in 1979 the company took over the U.S. distribution of mushroom spawn (seed) from Somycel, a firm based in France. In order to process the spawn, Monterey Mushrooms constructed the Amycel spawn plant at nearby San Juan Bautista and started production of spawn utilizing the finest mother cultures available from France and Switzerland. Next, in 1983 Monterey purchased three mushroom-growing facilities from Ralston-Purina, which were located in Morgan Hill, California; Madisonville, Texas; and Loudon, Tennessee, as well as a canning facility in Bonne Terre, Missouri.

As mushroom consumption per capita increased over the years, new opportunities for mushroom products began to develop. In 1985 Monterey began a new business that processed mushrooms from the fresh state into canned and frozen products. By adding value, these mushroom products were able to reach new consumers and satisfy market and customer needs. The Bonne Terre, Missouri, facility was converted to handle the new canned products, and a facility was leased in Santa Maria, California, to process the frozen mushroom products. Today Monterey's processed mushrooms can be found on salad bars, in restaurant meals, and in delis throughout the United States.

Even though the company was to see significant changes in its size and scope of operations because of these actions, its primary business remained the growing of mushrooms.

At first glance the concept of growing mushrooms seems simple enough: Take a few mushroom seeds, plant them in compost, and 13 weeks later, mushrooms. As with any agriculture product, there are many variables that can affect the quality and quantity of the mushroom harvest. And if quality and quantity are the requirements, then intense research and continuous monitoring are necessary. First, and foremost, a mushroom spawn is a microorganism that needs nutrition from several sources.

As a result, Monterey Mushrooms maintains state-of-the-art research laboratories at both its Prunedale and San Juan Bautista facilities that are fully staffed by qualified microbiologists and other professionals who keep track of the many intricacies of the mushroom and its environment. They want to know what the mushroom likes to eat, what makes it grow large, and what conditions best support its growth and maintenance.

In other words, the quality and quantity of the product is best ensured by maintaining tight control over all the variables during the time from spawn planting to harvest. It is the considered opinion of Monterey Mushrooms' management that, because the company does this well, it produces the finest-quality commercial mushrooms available in the United States.

In terms of what Monterey Mushrooms has meant to Santa Cruz County, the 277-acre Prunedale facility is the answer. There, at the largest aboveground growing facility in the United States, 600-plus employees are now responsible for the production of 25 to 30 million pounds of mushrooms per year. Although the facility is actually in Monterey County, most of the employees come from the Watsonville area. Likewise, most of the local businesses that benefit directly or indirectly from the Prunedale facility are in Santa Cruz County.

Today Monterey Mushrooms, with its corporate headquarters in Capitola, employs more than 2,000 people nationwide, has operations in seven states, is the largest mushroom grower and distributor in the United States, and sees annual revenues in excess of $100 million. Although one tends to associate the word "mushroom" with the word "slow," that is not the case with Monterey Mushrooms. At the Capitola executive offices the firm has an on-line computer system that gives it immediate access to all of its nationwide facilities. The company can monitor growing conditions, environmental status, corporate records, and marketing information, all within seconds. That is one example of the modern way to slowly and carefully grow and market mushrooms that will no doubt give Monterey Mushrooms the edge that will continue to make the firm an integral part of Santa Cruz County's future.

Monterey Mushrooms' Prunedale/Watsonville facility.

NATURIPE BERRY GROWERS

The Naturipe corporate offices in Watsonville.

The commercial growing of strawberries in the Pajaro Valley began in 1877, when James Waters planted 14 acres of the Cinderella variety on the Blackburn Ranch in Watsonville. Once picked, the strawberries were packed and shipped on the night train to San Francisco, where they drew the unbelievable price of 20 cents per pound. Based on these early beginnings a similar pattern was established for the distribution and sale between the growers in Watsonville and the commission houses in San Francisco that would go unchanged for the next 40 years.

By 1917 the local strawberry growers had long ago accepted the risks to their business from natural causes, but not those over which they had little control. These included overproduction, disorderly marketing, and the below-production "street" prices sometimes offered by the San Francisco commission houses that controlled the purse strings of the industry.

Thus, on April 9, 1917, 11 growers banded together, under the name of the Central California Berry Growers Association, and set out to correct the uncontrollable risks. Led by U. Shikuma, the association organized itself to collectively grow, pack, broker, and sell their own berries; develop new outlets; and advertise at the retail level. The organization's bylaws called for 10 directors, five to be Japanese-American and five to be Caucasian growers.

Although its ensuing history is much too large for this narrative, a few points should be mentioned. After the first year the group expanded to 248 members, representing 95 percent of the berry growers. In 1945 the Central California Berry Growers Association and the University of California Department of Plant Pathology jointly developed five new disease-resistant strawberry varieties with Naturipe as the industry leader. New University of California varieties are still the mainstay of today's industry, not only in California, but throughout the United States and the world. In the 1960s a university field station was established in Watsonville at Naturipe's insistence.

On March 4, 1922, the Central California Berry Growers Association adopted "Naturipe" as its official trademark. In 1958 the association was reorganized under the name Naturipe Berry Growers, with Herbert Baum as president. At that time Naturipe also expanded into Salinas, Anaheim, San Diego, and Oxnard.

Today Naturipe continues on much as it has for the past 70 years, except that now everything is moved by truck and the market is all over the United States. Currently Naturipe growers grow and distribute 7 million crates (12 pints to a crate) of fresh strawberries, using about 2,000 acres of land. They also market blackberries, raspberries, and peppers. In addition, Naturipe packs 40 million pounds of frozen berries for major companies in their own private labels, and the organization is the largest such packer in the world.

All processing, both fresh and frozen, is done at three separate locations: Oxnard, Anaheim, and Watsonville. Altogether, Naturipe Berry Growers employs about 1,000 people at these locations, and its headquarters remains in Watsonville to this day.

One of the first loads of strawberries ever to appear in the streets in San Francisco is seen here at the Fruit and Produce Commission Market about 1919. The berries had arrived the night before by train from the Oak Grove Berry Farm of Unosuke Shikuma, a founder of Naturipe. Members of the fourth generation of Shikuma's family are still involved with the association and serve on the board of directors.

PARTNERS IN PROGRESS

WATSONVILLE COMMUNITY HOSPITAL

Watsonville Community Hospital, while having roots dating back to 1894, is one of the most modern and technologically advanced acute care hospitals of its size in California. Examples of services performed by this 130-bed, well-staffed, nonprofit facility include quality inpatient care for local patients who stay an average of four and a half days, the yearly treatment of more than 26,000 people in its Emergency Center, and the routine handling of 200,000 laboratory procedures annually. Of course, it wasn't always like this.

It was back in November 1894 when Dr. Peter K. Watters rented a house on Beach Street, next to the old Opera House, and turned it into Watsonville's first hospital. Three years later he had a five-room facility built next to his residence on East Third Street. In 1902 Dr. Watters significantly expanded it by adding a larger building next door. At the same time he incorporated the new facility as the Watsonville Hospital and Training School for Nurses. In 1911 Dr. Henry Watters joined his father in practice at the hospital.

In 1926 Ehler Eiskamp, a graduate of Stanford University and the first doctor with surgical training in the Monterey Bay area, came to Watsonville. Fifty-seven years later, in 1983, he received the Rural Physician of the Year Award for California.

From 1923 until 1936 the day-to-day routine at the Watsonville Hospital continued. It was reported that at any one time 15 patients, staying at the rate of six dollars per day, could be found in the 13-room facility. In addition, there were six obstetrics rooms, a delivery room, and a nursery.

In 1937 Dr. Eiskamp, along with others in the community, realizing the need for a more modern institution, worked hard to raise $10,000 for such a facility. A site was located on Prospect Street, and by 1938 the new Watsonville Hospital was opened for business. For the next 30 years it served area needs.

In 1941 a nurse named Evelyn Craig joined the hospital staff. By 1947 she had became so good at so many things that, after taking hospital administration courses at Stanford University, she was appointed administrator of Watsonville Hospital. For many years thereafter Evelyn Craig and Dr. Eiskamp could be seen making daily rounds, caring for many local patients who remember them to this day.

In 1950 Watsonville Hospital incorporated as a nonprofit institution. As such, in the mid-1960s the staff, wanting to meet the community's expanding acute care needs, applied for and received a $2-million federal grant to help build a new facility. In addition, two successful fund-raising drives were carried out, and the modern four-story Watsonville Community Hospital became a reality in 1969. From the time of its first administrator, Irv Rosenthal, to M.G. Walser in 1970, to Bill Carpenter, who came on board in 1982, Watsonville Community Hospital has continued to expand and provide the best health care services available.

With the latest in services such as the Alcohol and Drug Treatment Program, cardiac catheterization, CT scanning, Family Birth Center, magnetic resonance imaging, mammography, Intensive Care Nursery, nuclear medicine, and outpatient surgery, Watsonville Community Hospital is definitely a Partner In Progress for Santa Cruz County.

Service League members volunteer countless hours working in the newly remodeled coffee shop and serving as unofficial hostesses for visitors and guests.

The personal touch of caring is offered by registered nurses and licensed vocational nurses at Watsonville Community Hospital.

BIG CREEK LUMBER COMPANY

Joshua Grinnell and Eddy Gifford in 1901. Gifford later became a professor of anthropology at U.C. Berkeley and is well known as the man who lived with and studied Ishi, one of the last California Indians.

Although seemingly a contradiction in terms, perhaps the premier environmentalists in Santa Cruz County today are Frank "Lud" McCrary, Jr., and his brother Homer "Bud" McCrary of the Big Creek Lumber Company. Not only were they born and raised on the lands they work, as were their parents and grandparents before them, but they have a deep respect for the land because it is a part of their very lives. Because they own 4,000 acres of forest-, ranch-, and farmlands along the north coast of Santa Cruz County; are lumbermen, working the Santa Cruz Mountains from Tunitas Creek near Half Moon Bay to Hecker Pass east of Watsonville; and are ranchers and farmers, raising cattle and horses, they are familiar with this Restless Paradise called Santa Cruz County. And not only are they familiar, but so are their children, some of whom are graduate foresters, who have chosen to work alongside their parents rather than somewhere else. Says Bud McCrary, "We're dedicated to the goal of keeping the forestry land forested. We buy land, but we've never sold any of it. We remove a lot of trees, but we never change the land's character." Continues Lud McCrary, "We want people to be able to utilize the land, but yet not abuse it. We don't want to see the place wall to wall houses."

In the early 1860s whaling captain Joshua Grinnell left California to return to Grinnell, Iowa, to see his family. In the spring of 1863, together with his wife, Elizabeth, and a five-year-old stepson, he returned west via wagon train. A year and a half later, allowing for a long stay in Carson City, Nevada, during one of its mineral booms, the family finally arrived in Santa Cruz County.

Setting up camp on the banks of the San Lorenzo River, at a place later to be known as Felton, Grinnell worked a couple of placer gold claims without much success. He then moved to the Meder Ranch on the coast side of the Ben Lomond Mountain Range. There he mined Hoy Creek (Majors Creek) and its tributaries for more than a year, finally discovering enough gold to satisfy him. In 1868 he was able to buy a 160-acre tract of land in Big Creek Canyon near Ingalls Station (Swanton), where he became a rancher and farmer. He later built a beautiful family house in a flat spot along Big Creek; his descendants, the McCrarys, still call it home.

The transition from ranching and farming to lumbering was inevitable. Ranching and farming in the steep and rocky Ben Lomond Coast Range of the Santa Cruz Mountains was, and is, a difficult and seasonal proposition. Thus, during off seasons, and because the woods were close by, many early ranchers and farmers learned how to cut split stuff, shakes and shingles, and board footage so they could make a little extra money.

So it was for Frank McCrary, Sr., and his brother in the 1920s and later during the Depression. Trying to make ends meet any way they could, they first operated a shingle mill and later a small sawmill at Felton. The mill would only handle 20-inch or smaller diameter saw logs, and it had a capacity of about 1,000 board feet of cut lumber per day. Still in all it worked, and for several years the McCrarys were able to cut lumber to make a profit.

Big Creek Lumber Company got its start after World War II when Frank McCrary, Sr.; his two sons, Lud and Bud;

Typical of the small lumbering operations in the days of Joshua Grinnell was this scene, depicting a bull team with a saw log going over a skid road for Isaiah Hartman.

and his brother-in-law, Homer Trumbo, formed a partnership. In 1946 the partners, using the old mill they nicknamed Termite, set out with crosscut saws and axes and worked portions of Mill and Scott creeks.

In 1947 Theodore Hoover (brother of Herbert Hoover) let it be known that he was interested in selling stumpage rights—rights to cut standing trees—on all of the land he owned in Waddell Creek Canyon. Intrigued with the idea,

The Big Creek Lumber Company's first mill on Waddell Creek.

the four men approached Hoover and attempted to acquire the rights. To their surprise a deal was struck—$4.50 per thousand board feet redwood and one dollar per thousand board feet Douglas fir—and the business was set to expand.

Soon thereafter the four drew up papers forming a partnership under the name Big Creek Timber Company. In short order they pooled the $3,000 in cash they had between them, started erecting a mill up Waddell Creek, bought two surplus Navy landing craft—out of which they took the two General Motors diesels to power the mill—and purchased a small D4 dozer to do the work. From the mill site the partners built several skid roads into the forest so the dozer could drag the cut saw logs back. In 1948 a small planing mill was built on the Pacific Coast Highway where the lumber from the mill was finished. In addition, as they worked further into Waddell Creek

The Big Creek Lumber Company mill on the ocean near Davenport, 1987.

Canyon, truck roads were built because it was too far for the dozer.

In 1955 one of the worst storms ever to hit California struck Waddell Creek Canyon. By the time it was over the truck roads had been washed out in five places, and other storm damage had occurred. Rather then rebuild, the partners decided to move the operation out to the planing mill site, the current location of the Big Creek Lumber Company.

Today, however, things are slightly different. The Big Creek Lumber Company mill cuts, planes, and processes 100,000 board feet of lumber per day. The current mill has two separate head rig saws that can handle saw logs coming in on the carriage from six feet down to six inches in diameter. Lasers are used to draw guide lines on the precut slabs so the edgermen can make precise cuts. Today 95 percent of the trees processed are redwoods, and the balance are Douglas fir and Monterey pine. In addition to the north coast facility, Big Creek also has yards in Watsonville and Paso Robles. The firm maintains a fleet of log and lumber trucks to transport raw material from woods to mill, and to deliver the finished product to customers. Big Creek has 170 full-time employees at its three locations.

As of now there are more trees in the forest than when the first loggers began cutting them in Santa Cruz County. Because Big Creek Lumber Company practices selective harvesting, 70 percent of the saleable volume of a given tract can be harvested by cutting less than 50 percent of the trees. When a thick clump of redwood trees is thinned, the remaining trees grow much faster, and sprouts will develop from the cut stumps and grow as much as 10 feet in the first year. Lud and Bud McCrary like to point this out because the forest is better today than when they first started with their dad and uncle. Today, from the stump of the first tree that Lud McCrary and Homer Trumbo cut by hand, sprouts a 30-inch-diameter, 150-foot-tall Sequoia sempervirens redwood.

ROSES OF YESTERDAY AND TODAY

Sometimes the pursuit of history leads researchers into areas not normally thought of by many as historical in nature. Yet many times just such research can have a powerful impact on the history of man himself. So it is for the people at Roses of Yesterday and Today in Watsonville, whose entire business is based on the history of old, rare, unusual, and selected modern roses. For more than 40 years they have taken pride in historically selecting, growing, and selling 230 different varieties of the finest bareroot rose plants available anywhere in the world. Some of these plants, like Rosa Damascena Bifera, have a history that dates back to before Christ.

I am prejudiced in these roses' favor . . . I am prejudiced in favor of Dorothy Stemler, who is, by those having long rose-growing dealings with her, apt to be regarded as something of a rose herself. I like, I love my prejudices.
James Gould Cozzens
Roses of Yesterday (1967)

It was 1945 when Dorothy Stemler made the decision to leave Riverside, California, with her young son and daughter and pursue a longtime dream. For years she had studied the history of roses, and she had successfully grown several varieties as a hobby. Now that she was divorced and on her own, she would turn her hobby into a livelihood.

Shortly before this an old English gardener, Francis Lester, and his wife had come to live in the Monterey Bay area. After a short time they discovered a beautiful little spot of coolness, meandering stream, and giant redwoods nestled deep in the foothills of the Santa Cruz Mountains. The area was locally known as Brown's Valley. There Lester decided to build a home and a nursery. He started growing everything from blackberries to

Dorothy Stemler, world-renowned rose authority, who turned her love of roses into a livelihood.

daffodils to a few old roses. Before long he found himself in partnership with a previous acquaintance, Will Tillotson, who shared his interest. Soon Lester and Tillotson were growing, warehousing, and selling several thousand bareroot rose plants per year. Tillotson especially had a love for roses, and in later years he made it his life's work, traveling all over the world to collect the various plants.

As the business began to expand Lester and Tillotson had need for some additional help. Tillotson had known a lady, Dorothy Stemler, who had a lot of knowledge about roses and used to work for him

The offices of Roses of Yesterday and Today, shaded from view by a giant redwood tree, overlooks the garden.

in Riverside when he was an orange shipper. He contacted her and asked if she would like to get into the rose business. Dorothy Stemler arrived with her children in Brown's Valley, took up a house a short distance from the nursery, and began a new life looking after the cares and concerns of a rose business.

As Dorothy soon found out, the business was not large enough to support her family and herself on a full-time basis. As a result, she had to take a job in Watsonville during the day as a law secretary for the Wyckoff law firm. At night she continued working for Lester and Tillotson, doing everything from book work to order filling to the cutting of the scion buds.

In 1948 Lester died. For a short time after that Tillotson was in partnership with Mrs. Lester. In 1951 Tillotson became sole proprietor of the business. For the next six years Roses of Yesterday and Today continued to grow under the careful guidance of Tillotson and Dorothy Stemler. By the end of this period 20,000 bareroot rose plants were being grown and sold annually. In 1957 Tillotson died while in England. Because of Dorothy Stemler's love of the flowers, and because she had done everything for him from photography to cutting the budwood for the field, he willed her the fledgling business.

And so it went. Roses of Yesterday and Today, under the loving care of Dorothy Stemler, with the assistance of her daughter, Patricia, would continue to grow in both size and stature. Over the next 19 years Dorothy would become a world-renowned rose authority. She would write two books, *The Book of Old Roses* (1966) and *Roses of Yesterday* (1967), and she would produce yearly catalogs. Eventually she would come to be known as the "The Lady of Old Roses." Today, in her honor, the American Rose Society perpetually awards the Dorothy C. Stemler Memorial Award at the National Spring Rose Show for the Best Old Rose Bouquet entered.

In 1976 the reins of Roses of Yester-

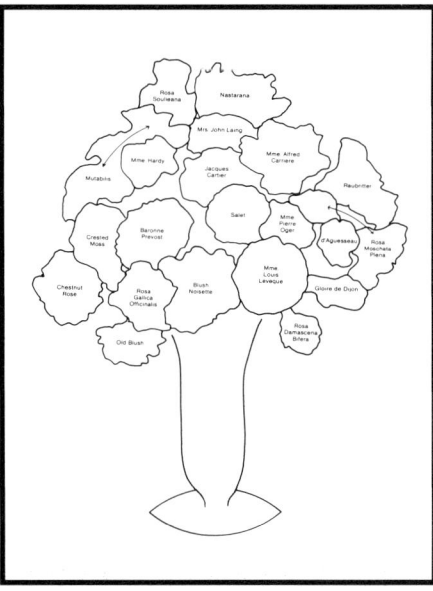

day and Today passed to her longtime helpmate and daughter, Patricia. Even though she was married and looking after six children, Patricia would carry on in the tradition of her mother, because of her own love of the roses.

Today Roses of Yesterday and Today is a family corporation. Patricia Wiley is president; her husband, Newton Wiley, is vice-president; her only daughter, Kathryn Minier, is secretary; Kathryn's husband, Tryg, handles packing and shipping; and Patricia's five sons, Newton, Richard, Thomas, Jack, and Joel, make up the board of directors. From fledgling beginnings has come a company that sells and ships between 100,000 and 150,000 retail bareroot rose plants per year.

Surprisingly, as Patricia Wiley points out, "The plants themselves are currently grown in McFarland, about 35 miles north of Bakersfield. This is necessary because the coastal climate is too temperate and too warm. You have to go where the rose can go dormant in the fall, and McFarland usually sees an early frost." When ready, the rose plants are shipped from McFarland to the Brown's Valley-Watsonville facility, where they are kept in cold storage, at 37 degrees Fahrenheit, and then shipped from January to May in a dormant condition.

Like her mother, Dorothy, Patricia is

To know roses is to love them. Here are several old favorites in a classic bouquet and a key to their names (left).

a recognized rose authority around the world. In 1987 she was a guest speaker at the International Rose Conference in Australia. She also gave a seminar at the Kisei Rose Research Institute in Japan. Closer to home, she is a member of the Monterey Bay Area Rose Society, which holds open house in the beautiful gardens of Roses of Yesterday and Today each Mother's Day.

As to the future, only time will tell. Will daughter Kathy, who currently lives in the original family house of her grandmother, follow in the family footsteps? To quote Patricia, "This business could not run very efficiently without Kathy's constant help and knowledge. She has absorbed a surprising amount of understanding about the roses and their personalities in her years of working with them."

One thing is certain. The love of the rose is everywhere visible at Roses of Yesterday and Today. Likewise, one has only to look at the prices in the company's current 80-page catalog to realize that the love of the rose is still far more important than the dollar in the pocket.

SANTA CRUZ COUNTY

DEL MAR FOODS

Perhaps Wayne Jordan of Del Mar Foods best described what being a Partner in Progress is all about when he referred to the Wastsonville area as a "synergy." First and foremost Watsonville is at the center of the major fruit and vegetable growing valleys in California. As a result, it is there that most of the raw agricultural product comes to be processed, packaged, and sold in its final form of frozen, canned, or fresh merchandise. Thus, Watsonville is where the major U.S. customers come to buy, and where several trucking firms and one of the largest railroads in the country daily service the needs of these buyers and sellers. Finally, Watsonville is a place where growers, processors, packagers, sellers, distributors, customers, storage concerns, shippers, transportation companies, and all those people who work for them, cooperatively come together to help feed much of America.

Because Watsonville also happens to be the largest frozen-food processing center in the United States, freezing and cold-storage companies such as Del Mar Foods play an active role in this synergy. Says current president P.J. Mecozzi, "We are tied to this community in that we depend on the local growers. We are also a customer-driven organization in that everyone is working for the customer. Because of our commitments in both directions we have been allowed to survive in this very tumultuous industry. We have one plant here. We live here. We're committed to Watsonville."

Del Mar Foods' prime business involvements include the freezing of fruit indigenous to the Watsonville area and a related cold-storage and freezing enterprise on the same property. Every year 150 full-time employees, plus 300 more during peak seasons, working on up to four different lines at the same time, are responsible for the production of 30 million pounds of various frozen fruit. At the same time Del Mar Foods' cold-storage enterprise provides up to 1.2 million cubic feet of freezer space for other local freezing companies. Altogether, this 12-acre facility, with its 70,000-square-foot processing and packaging plant and its 45,000 square feet of cold-storage space, is a major component of the Watsonville area frozen-food business.

However, when Al Smith first got the idea for Del Mar Foods back in the early 1950s, he probably didn't realize just how big it would become. Smith was born and raised on a ranch in the Santa Clara Valley. As a young man he went to work for the local canneries. Later he moved south to Los Angeles where he was employed by the Simple-Simon Pie Company (Norton-Simon). He didn't work there very long before he realized the need for frozen fruit

Apples pass along the line on their way to being sliced and frozen.

114

It's strawberry processing time on the evening line at Del Mar Foods.

so pies could be made year round. He also realized there was a need to make the pies closer to the source of raw product. In 1957 he left Simple-Simon and moved to Soquel where he started a small business, processing and freezing local fruit under the name of Del Mar Foods. Unfortunately, after two successful years, he was to lose almost everything in a fire.

Undaunted, Smith started again in 1959 in a leased processing plant in Watsonville belonging to John Mello. John—the father of current state senator Henry Mello—had had the facility for several years, along with a cold-storage unit, which he routinely leased out to anyone who wanted to process a particular crop. While Smith was definitely a man of the land, a good manager, and a genius with machinery, he was also short on funds at the time. In 1961 he was about to go under when D.B. Berelson and Charles Buchwald provided reorganizing solvency in the form of partners. Shortly thereafter the company took off under Smith's management, and there was no slowing down for the next 15 years. Smith died unexpectedly in 1976; Berelson and Buchwald remain affiliated with Del Mar Foods to this day.

John Tipton, who started with Del Mar Foods back in 1963, relates that the early 1960s were good years for the firm. During that period Del Mar Foods was primarily an apple company. Not only was Del Mar peeling, cutting, slicing, and freezing fillers for other corporations, but it was also in the business of making pies for Morton. Recalls Tipton, "We used to run 100 pies a minute, or from 30,000 to 50,000 pies per day."

By 1973 Del Mar Foods had grown to the extent that the firm reorganized and bought the facilities it had been leasing. At the same time the company purchased the cold-storage units next door from Henry Mello to better serve its future needs. It should be noted that this reorganization also involved a change in management philosophy. Up until the oil embargo of 1972 Del Mar Foods had been able to ship apples east at the freight rate of two cents per pound and effectively compete with eastern grower/shipper groups. By the time the embargo was over the freight rate had gone to nine cents per pound, and the eastern market was lost.

As a result, the decision was made to expand the company's product line to include strawberries and peaches. To this day those three products each represent about 30 percent of Del Mar Foods' total business. In addition, the firm also processes apricots, olallie berries (a strain of blackberry), and red and green bell peppers. The majority of what Del Mar processes is sold to companies such as Westco, Campbell, and S.E. Rykoff, and to the baking industry for further processing.

Today president P.J. Mecozzi and general manager Wayne Jordan are the individuals most heavily involved in the organization's future. And they have a lot to build on. Most of Del Mar Foods' product is now individually quick frozen (IQF) using carbon dioxide gas applied directly to the fruit. Wayne Jordan, who has been with the firm for more than 20 years, says, "This is by far the most superior method of freezing in terms of preserving the product. Because it only takes 10 minutes to accomplish, the food will taste better and have more eye appeal when the product is served. Also, unlike the old 24-hour refrigerated method, this requires far less energy."

Where before energy was only a minor element in the cost of production, it is the major component today. Because the freezing of food is such an energy-intensive industry, costs have to be cut wherever possible. Today the fruit to be processed arrives at Del Mar Foods all day long, where it is stored and allowed to naturally cool into early evening. This brings the internal ambient temperature of the fruit down. The fruit is then processed at night when it is cooler, thereby requiring less energy to freeze the product. Night processing also brings a better energy rate.

It is innovative planning such as this that allows Del Mar Foods to be competitive in an unfair marketplace—unfair in that much of today's competition is from foreign countries that provide subsidies to their processors. Thus, they undercut U.S. industry prices.

For Del Mar Foods the future, like the past, remains a delicate balance within the synergy of Watsonville. Tipton is quick to point out: "I grew up on a ranch, and that was my background. This business is an extension of that background. It starts in the field and goes right on through. I don't think the youngsters of today with their business degrees have that tie to the ground. Therefore, it will be harder for them." Says Mecozzi, "We are a commodity packer that must remain competitive. We have served our customers well as a quality producer. As such, we will continue to grow as they grow."

J.J. CROSETTI CO., INC.

Congressional Record, 96th Congress, Second Session, Volume Number 176, Washington, 12, 1980, House of Representatives:

"Mr. Panetta." "Mr. Speaker. J.J. 'Joe' Crosetti is an accomplished agribusinessman, musician, and benefactor of just causes who has played a major role in the growth and development of the city of Watsonville and the county of Santa Cruz, California. His accomplishments are legion, his counsel sought after, and his friendship treasured by those fortunate enough to know him. I proudly count myself among those who call him friend."

What followed was the reading of an editorial from the Watsonville *Register-Pajaronian* about a man of the soil, his life, his success in the fresh produce business, and his 50 years of service to his community. Among other things mentioned: Joe Crosetti was chairman of the local Red Cross for 42 years and a director and six-term chairman of the County Fair Board for 40 years. As an agribusinessman he was a longtime director and periodic chairman of three separate associations: the Central California Grower-Shipper Vegetable Association, the Western Growers' Association, and the California-Arizona Growers' Association.

Joe Crosetti graduated from Watsonville High School in 1927. He was a local boy, following in the footsteps of his Italian father who had first come to the Pajaro Valley in 1898. Next to the land, Joe's greatest love was music. An accomplished saxophone player, he started his adult life by joining a ship's orchestra and traveling all over the world. Crosetti soon returned to the land, however, when he took a job with local produce shipper Tim Horgan. From there he went to work as a field salesman for the wholesale produce firm of Levi-Zentner, "calling on all the Italian buyers up the coast."

The year 1935 was to be a turning point in Joe Crosetti's life: That was the year he married Theresa Muzzio and decided to form his own company. Crosetti started with tomatoes and later went to lettuce. His initial business consisted of advancing money to the grower and then, after packing and selling the produce, he would split the profits with the grower.

By 1940, in addition to fixed packing facilities, Crosetti had his own vacuum processing plant, mounted on two rail flatcars, which he moved from one growing area to another. At one time 6,000 acres of lettuce per year were being processed in this manner in the Imperial, Salinas, and Pajaro valleys. In the 1950s Crosetti expanded into other row crops such as broccoli and cauliflower. Eventually all three products were strong marketing items.

In addition to the J.J. Crosetti Co., Inc., fresh vegetable outlet, Joe also founded the Crosetti Orchards Co. As the freezing of certain row crops became a natural extension of the business, Crosetti Frozen Foods was incorporated in 1966. Before Joe Crosetti fell prey to ill health in 1979, these three separate companies, along with thousands of acres of producing Crosetti fields and orchards, would be the result of the efforts of one man—Joe Crosetti.

Today, with Joe in retirement, J.J. Crosetti, Jr., oversees the three operations. While fresh vegetables are still distributed, and 150 acres of red delicious and pippin apples are picked each year, the prime business emphasis has become frozen foods. Each year more than 65 million pounds of various vegetables are processed by 600 local employees and then sold to major customers worldwide. Ninety percent of the products end up with institutional consumers such as hospitals, the military, national wholesale distributors, and restaurants. Says J.J. Crosetti, Jr., "Although people don't see our label, if you eat in restaurants, at one time or another, you've eaten our product."

At one time the name Joe Crosetti was synonymous with lettuce.

FILICE DISTRIBUTORS

Bruno Filice, Sr. (fourth from left), is surrounded by the Filice Distributors "family."

Although Filice Distributors is a relatively young firm in terms of Santa Cruz County, the roots of its founders go back a long way in the business itself. Bruno and Frank Filice grew up in the lower Santa Clara Valley, where their family had owned and operated the San Martin Winery since 1933. As the boys grew into adulthood, they were taken into the wine business and remained actively involved in the San Martin Winery until the family sold it in 1972. While Bruno moved on, Frank stayed with the management group of the winery to help the new owners.

In 1975 Bruno opened a new type of business, the Watsonville Travel Agency. As he needed a rest from the hectic demands of the distribution business, his plan was to both work and play at the same time. He did just that for the next three years until a new opportunity presented itself.

In 1978 the Santa Cruz County Coors beer distributorship went on the market. Bruno and Frank were anxious to get back into the distribution game. Thus, Bruno turned the travel agency over to his capable wife and daughter, and acquired the Coors franchise. Along with his brother Frank, he set out to make Coors the number-one beer in the county. To make a long story short, they have progressed to the point where Coors is now number two and gaining. They have done so well, in fact, that in 1985 the Adolph Coors Company selected Filice Distributors to receive its highest award for distributor excellence, the Founder's Award.

To talk about Filice Distributors is to also talk about the family that runs it. Over the years Bruno has brought his sons, Mark and Bruno Jr., into the business. Likewise, Frank has sons Dean, Darin, and Steve involved. In addition, nephews Jerry Wiens and David Bruni and niece Janice Williams are part of the work force. Together they form the nucleus of Filice Distributors. To quote Bruno Filice, regarding the workaday world of a family-run beer distributorship, "In the beer business the turnover (of product) is very fast, which at times gets quite hectic. Sometimes tempers flare, but we're all family. We forget it, and we still break bread together afterward."

Filice Distributors currently occupies 25,000 square feet of floor space in two buildings and has 21 full-time employees looking after its sales, distribution, and office management. It maintains a rail siding where Coors beer is brought in by refrigerated freight car from Golden, Colorado, and it operates a fleet of trucks that deliver product from Davenport to southeast of Watsonville. In addition to Coors beer and its new products—Herman Joseph and Extra Gold—Filice Distributors also sells and distributes Henry Weinhard, Moosehead, California Cooler, Crystal Geyser Water, Sapporo beer, Pacifico beer, Orangina, Rainier Ale, Hidleburg, Black Label, and Kronanburg. As a community service a recycling center operates three days a week where the firm takes back all types of aluminum cans and Coors glass bottles.

In summing up Filice Distributors, Bruno probably put it best when he said: "We are a family-oriented business. We try to develop a friendship, a closeness, with our accounts. We are there to give the best-possible service and treat each account as a member of our family." In particular, "We are Italians, and family is the Italian way. We want to treat the whole city and county of Santa Cruz as our adopted family."

AMI COMMUNITY HOSPITAL OF SANTA CRUZ

AMI Community Hospital of Santa Cruz Mission Statement:

"The primary mission of AMI Community Hospital of Santa Cruz is to provide high-quality, cost-effective medical care with the help of a staff of capable physicians and medical professionals. Caring is our mission."

In achieving the goals of its mission, AMI Community Hospital of Santa Cruz is a full-service, general acute care facility. Services include: a 24-hour, 7-day-a-week emergency department; obstetrical department with alternative birthing centers; an intensive and coronary care unit; and pediatric, medical, and surgical departments. While the parent corporation is the second-largest health care system in the United States and is international in scope with more than 110 hospitals worldwide, each local facility is still dedicated to total individual patient care in every respect. In look-

It is AMI Community Hospital's philosophy that "when high technology is combined with high touch, the result is quality patient care, care that is second to none."

ing at AMI Community Hospital of Santa Cruz today, it is hard to believe it came from the small health care facility originally built 28 years ago.

In the late 1960s several local doctors saw the need for a private hospital in Santa Cruz. Before long the idea gathered momentum, and a prominent local businessman,

AMI Community Hospital of Santa Cruz opened in 1959 as a privately funded, 49-bed facility. Today it is a full-service, general acute care, 180-bed facility.

Harald Sundean, stepped forth and provided the necessary funding. After a year of construction the new single-wing, 49-bed Community Hospital opened the doors to its first patient on October 1, 1959.

As the community began to expand and more people moved into the Santa Cruz area, the need for additional services and a larger facility became evident. In 1968 a new 50-bed addition was completed and open for patients.

As 1970 approached, Santa Cruz County found itself in a phenomenal growth pattern; because of this the county government was starting to have trouble funding the county hospital, and signs indicated it wouldn't be long before that facility might be closing its doors. Also, the field of electronic medicine had recently seen unbelievable advances in research and diagnostic apparatus. As a result, it soon became apparent that an even larger hos-

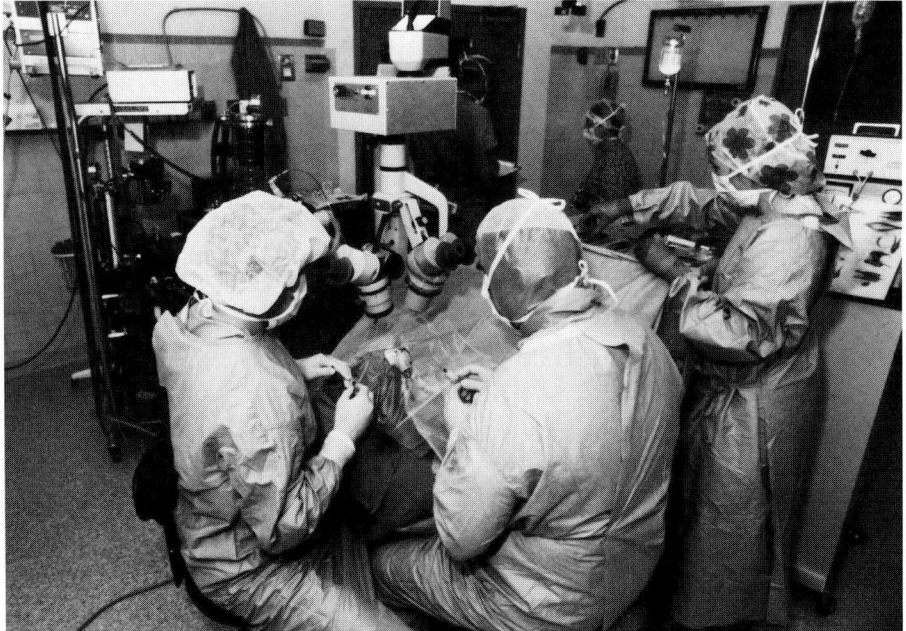

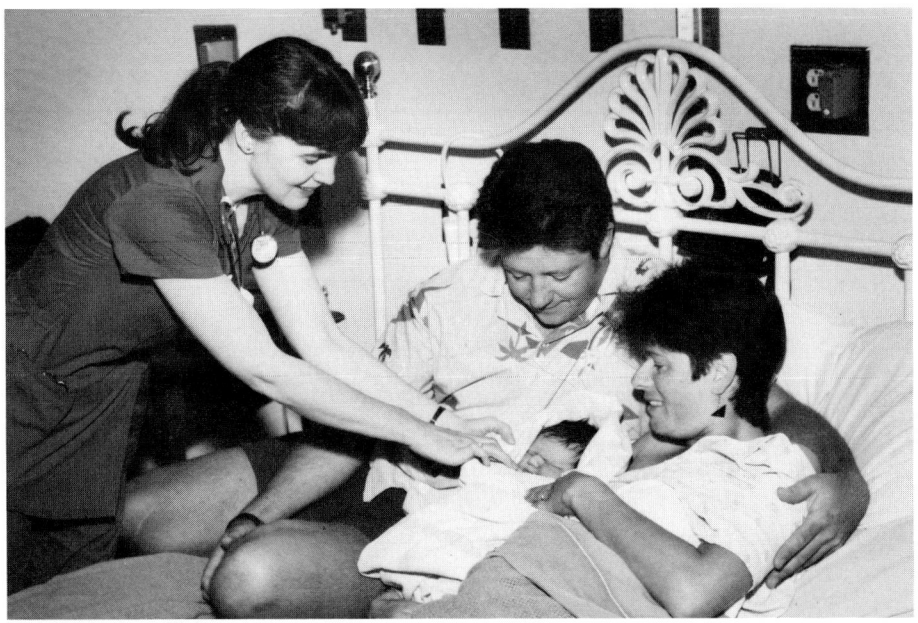

AMI Community Hospital of Santa Cruz established the first alternative birth center in the Santa Cruz community in 1977. The center gives the comfort of a home-like delivery and enables family participation while also providing the security of a licensed physician and emergency facilities.

pital with more beds and the latest medical technologies was needed if the medical community was to keep up with the increased demand for local health care.

In 1971 construction began on a new three-story wing of the hospital that would bring to the Santa Cruz community state-of-the-art health care. By the end of the year the building was in place and the planned upgrading of services begun. First, a fully equipped and well staffed intensive care unit (ICU) was established. By 1972 extra space was made available for 80 additional beds.

Recognizing the varied life-styles and philosophies of Santa Cruz County residents, the hospital established the first, unique alternative birth center in 1977. Under the direction of Dr. Joseph D'Amico, a program was established for prospective parents who wanted the comfort of a home delivery and family participation, but did not want to sacrifice the security of a nearby emergency facility and a licensed physician. As a result, several well-designed rooms, with home-like decor, were provided in the maternity ward where fathers could stay around the clock and where other family members could be present during natural labor, delivery, and recovery. If for some unforeseen reason complications should arise, a full maternity staff is at the ready to provide all necessary emergency medical and/or surgical care.

In 1979 American Medical International (AMI) bought the hospital, changing its name to AMI Community Hospital of Santa Cruz. This was a significant gain for the local area because it meant that Community Hospital could bring major educational and material resources of a much larger health care system and management to the community. Under the new management, an in-depth review of the facility was carried out. The plans laid brought the hospital the latest high-tech medical services, while providing for individualized patient care. It is AMI Community Hospital's philosophy that "when high technology is combined with high touch, the result is quality patient care, care that is second to none."

Over the past 10 years AMI Community Hospital of Santa Cruz has done much to achieve quality patient care. Shortly after the hospital became an AMI facility, the emergency department was remodeled, and some of the most sophisticated monitoring equipment available was installed. Next, a new Intensive Care/Coronary Care Unit of the most advanced design was completed. Coupled with this was a Critical Care Nurses program that allowed specific opportunities for a nurse to plan, implement, and follow his/her patient's care from admission to discharge. In 1985 AMI Community Hospital introduced phase one of its strategic plan for the first heart program in Santa Cruz County by opening a Cardiac Catheterization Laboratory. Phase two of this heart program began in 1987 with the initiation of open heart surgery. The Santa Cruz Heart Institute, located at AMI Community Hospital of Santa Cruz, is a comprehensive, fully integrated, central resource for heart health care and is designed to exclusively diagnose and treat cardiovascular diseases.

Today AMI Community Hospital of Santa Cruz continues to provide full-service diagnostic and therapeutic capabilities. The hospital's emergency department, linked to both city and county paramedics, can treat anything from a minor accident to a major trauma. The obstetrical department is adding an Intensive Care Nursery, and other medical, surgical, and pediatric services are expanding.

AMI Community Hospital of Santa Cruz, a leader in the health care industry, is committed to the community it serves. Contributions such as the establishment of a nonprofit foundation for the sole purpose of community educational programs, and the ability to attract and sustain well-trained and educated professionals, are some of the ways the hospital strives to heighten the quality of life for the community. Responsive professional attention, the most advanced medical technology, and progressive health care programs geared to the individual are all necessary ingredients of a community of caring—a community formed by the hospital and medical staff of AMI Community Hospital of Santa Cruz.

THE RAILROADS OF F. NORMAN CLARK

A boy of 14 slowly gazed in amazement across the massive turntable to the roundhouse at Goldfield, Nevada, to watch the many steam locomotives being brought to life for the day's assignments. Almost immediately an indelible image of past and present western history began to etch itself into his memory forever.

Ten years later the boy, now a vibrant young man, returned to Goldfield only to find the railroad, and all that had been connected with it, gone. All that remained was the indelible image of 10 years previous and the dream to have it back. Ironically, because of that image, it was at that specific point in time that F. Norman Clark realized he would spend the rest of his life preserving, restoring, and operating antique railroad equipment and recreating associated western history, so that future generations could get a glimpse of the past.

In 1959, after being fascinated by an article in *Pacific News* magazine by Karl Koenig about the famed Santa Cruz Branch of the South Pacific Coast, Norman Clark found himself soon walking along the remaining 10-mile portion still operated by the Southern Pacific. Imagine, he thought, what it must have been like back in the 1870s, when the Santa Cruz & Felton used to operate its pristine little narrow gauge lumber trains through these

A dapper, winterized F. Norman Clark, with pin in hand, is about to link up the narrow gauge Kahuku *to its passenger car.*

giant redwoods from the flume head down to waiting ships in Monterey Bay. And then there was the fanciful South Pacific Coast, financed entirely by Comstock millionaire James Fair, which took the Santa Cruz & Felton over in the 1880s and made it part of its line between Alameda and Santa Cruz. What a time it must have been, when diminutive passenger and freight trains roamed the lush Santa Cruz Mountains to the delight of tourist and entrepreneur alike. Later, over the same route, the predecessor Southern Pacific operated larger and longer standard gauge trains, pulled by mammoth double-headed, steam locomotives for over 30 years. "If only I could go back and recapture that time," dreamed Norman Clark.

Shortly thereafter, he went to the Southern Pacific and asked if it would consider selling him the infrequently used line. The company's emphatic answer was no. Because the dream kept gnawing at him, however, he would return every six months, again and again, only to receive the same definite no.

Roaring Camp & Big Trees Narrow Gauge Railroad

While trying unsuccessfully to negotiate with the Southern Pacific, Clark spent considerable time walking around in Henry Cowell Park. During that time he became aware of a 180-acre tract of land, belonging to Margaret Coolidge, that was in the redwood forest but not part of the park itself. He soon realized that if he modified his dream slightly, he could build a typical 1880s narrow gauge lumbering railroad and a western logging camp, all within the boundaries of the Welch property. It would start at the original SPC Felton depot in the beautiful Ley Meadow,

A finer stable of narrow gauge logging locomotives never graced a western railroad engine house.

travel up some of the steepest grades imaginable, traverse unbelievably tight curves around monstrous redwood trees that were too big to move, cross over high wooden trestles, and end up at a point 4.5 miles distant and several hundred feet higher in elevation.

In 1960, with $25 in his pocket and after a full year of negotiations with Margaret and Glen Coolidge, Clark was able to incorporate the Roaring Camp & Big Trees Narrow Gauge Railroad, complete with 99-year lease on the property. On April 6, 1963, the first narrow gauge passenger train to leave the Felton Depot in 56 years departed for the Big Trees Grove. On April 2, 1966, the railroad was completed and service began to Bear Mountain. Shortly thereafter, construction began on the western town of Roaring Camp where initially a mercantile, depot, school, sawmill, rail car soda fountain, and bookstore would

A typical summer day at the beach finds a crowded Suntan Special arriving and discharging its eager passengers.

Various members of F. Norman Clark's railroads with the first train to the Santa Cruz Boardwalk. On top are brakeman Marc Desobeau and engineer Vaughn Lamb with (bottom, left to right) Mike DiDonato, vice-president; Georgiana Clark, president; Jack Hanson, conductor; Karl Koenig, engineer and western writer; Phil Reader, brakeman; and Tom Shreve, steam engineer.

reside.

Today, some 22 years later, Norman Clark's railroad, simply known as Roaring Camp, is an established fact. There 35 employees are devoted to using old technologies and preserving the past on one of the finest examples of narrow gauge railroading left in the United States.

Santa Cruz, Big Trees & Pacific Railway

One particularly bad night in 1982 it started to rain in Santa Cruz County. Before it was over major portions of the Southern Pacific Santa Cruz-Big Trees line had been washed away. For months thereafter the line sat idle. Finally the railroad decided to abandon rather than fix the line. And guess who was at the One Market Street, San Francisco, front door asking the railroad executives if they would sell it? After three years of negotiations, Clark unbelievably found himself president of a 10-mile railway, to be known as the Santa Cruz, Big Trees & Pacific.

On October 12, 1985, the new railroad made its inaugural 2.5-mile run from Roaring Camp to Rincon. The line was still to be repaired from there to Santa Cruz. Clark vowed, however, that his train would be in town, all the way to the beach, by the following spring. Unfortunately, while working side by side with his employees during several cold winter days, he caught a cold he couldn't shake. The cold developed into pneumonia, and he died from the effects, never to see his original dream come true.

Undaunted, his wife, Georgiana Clark, assumed the presidency and picked up where he left off. On July 4, 1986, after much work by her stalwart track crews, the first revenue passenger train arrived at the Sashmill on the outskirts of Santa Cruz. On September 6 the line was opened to the original 1893 downtown Union Depot. Finally, on October 12, Norman Clark's dream became a reality. At 10:30 a.m., behind modern diesel equipment using antique 1902 wooden and early 1926 steel coaches, the first run of the new Suntan Special to the beach at Santa Cruz was completed.

Today anyone can board historic trains at Roaring Camp or Santa Cruz and once again experience the ride in either open-air or enclosed passenger cars behind steam and diesel locomotives typical of the different eras. Both the Roaring Camp & Big Trees Narrow Gauge Railroad and the Santa Cruz, Big Trees & Pacific Railway are primarily in business to help people relax and once again become acquainted with another time in western railroad history. Thank you, F. Norman Clark.

GEO. H. WILSON, INC.

Geo. H. Wilson, Inc., is a family-owned mechanical contracting firm that evolved through hard work and dedication from the original partnership of Izant and Wilson. Geo. H. Wilson devoted all his energies toward developing a successful business with a reputation for quality work. The following text provides a glimpse of the founder's life and the evolution of his company.

"My father started out a schoolteacher, later going into business, operating retail stores. Serious fire losses, health problems, my mother's death, and more convinced him to move to California where he became a one-man California chamber of commerce.

"I came to Santa Cruz from Wisconsin in the fall of 1899—apples on the ground, trees losing leaves—with grandmother (80), three sisters (10, 8, and 3), and myself (6), on the train. Grandma brought a big basket filled with bread and stuff to eat, and we lived on it for the week as we were on the train crossing the country. The one-room school we went to for two years was actually on our ranch in Doyle (now Rodeo) Gulch. We moved after several years into town because dad found out he wasn't a rancher. I went to Mission Hill School, then Santa Cruz High School for two years.

"In 1909 I went to work at a dollar a day for the Pilkington brothers, who were starting a plumbing and metal shop in Seabright—working on and off at various jobs—until World War I. After two years as a sergeant in the Motor Transport Corps, I returned in 1919 to Santa Cruz and applied to Byrne Brothers, a leading hardware and plumbing firm, for employment. Mr. Bert H. Izant, a partner in the firm in charge of contracting, employed me at $5.40 per day. Never having worked at high wages and under union conditions before, and afraid of getting fired (due to forgetting how to work), I worked overtime. I found out I had not forgotten how and was made foreman of the plumbing department after a few months. One-and-one-half years later Mr. Izant, 15 years my senior, and I formed a partnership. It lasted exactly 25 years, from March 1, 1921, until March 1, 1946, when Mr. Izant retired.

"Starting with a capital of $3,000, we purchased a used Model T Ford with a small box on the back minus a rear fender, but which turned out to be a jewel. We drove to San Francisco, through Chittenden Pass and Gilroy, the long way (the Glenwood Highway was incomplete at this time), to get our first tools and supplies, and to establish credit. We returned three days later, the little Ford loaded to the axles, with no breakdown. This Ford continued to be our main source of transportation for the next four or five years.

Ninety-four-year-old Geo. H. Wilson poses for a recent photograph at his home.

"We rented the building on the corner of Water and Bulkhead, formerly a blacksmith shop and then a feed store, which the owner remodeled for our operation. We used the building for the next 32 years (25 as Izant & Wilson and seven as Geo. H. Wilson).

"Starting as a two-man team, Mr. Izant did the sheet metal and I the plumbing. We operated like this for several months before hiring any help. We worked for years, primarily on residential homes. Prior to the early 1940s there were no planning commissions and very few construction inspection services. Contractors of all different crafts, with few exceptions, took pride in building their reputations. In 1946, the year Mr. Izant retired, we each were drawing $250 per month, an excellent salary, for everything we could want."

Thus Geo. H. Wilson relates the firm's early years.

About the time that Wilson became a single entrepreneur, the town of Santa Cruz began to grow. Schools and commercial structures began to be built, and they all needed plumbing. Pretty soon Geo. H. Wilson, Inc., found itself getting into

The firm of Izant & Wilson and its fleet of trucks in the early 1930s.

heavier work and bigger projects. In 1950 Jim Wilson, son of George, joined the firm to help out. Also, George's wife, "Wave," quickly became a regular fixture around the office, exercising her unique skills wherever needed. By 1952 the original location had become so crowded that the business moved to the current facility at 125 River Street. It would be from this point on that Geo. H. Wilson, Inc., would begin to see less residential work and more large-scale work.

By 1971, about the time George Wilson could take a few days off every once in a while, the business was expanding rapidly with growth in the Santa Clara Valley.

Currently the firm of Geo. H. Wilson, Inc., considers itself a mechanical contractor. According to grandson Tom, who works with his brother Richard and their father, Jim, "We do industrial plumbing, heating, sheet metal, air conditioning, refrigeration, water systems, custom stainless steel, and architectural sheet metal." If, however, a special fitting or other odd part is needed, a retail counter is featured that will sell any of those items accumulated over the past 67 years of business.

Today Geo. H. Wilson, Inc., employs from 100 to 150 people at any one time, depending on the work load. Its gross volume routinely exceeds $10 million per year. Ironically, most of the job sites are out of Santa Cruz County; however, much of the fabrication and assembly work is still done locally with state-of-the-art equipment. Recent achievements include the revamped facilities for the Santa Cruz Seaside Company, Synertek, the Lone Star emission-control systems, upgrades at Wrigley and Lipton food-processing plants, the Lockheed Missiles & Space test site on Ben Lomond Mountain, and the new Hewlett-Packard offices at the Mayfield Mall.

And so it goes. The man who drove

State-of-the-art mechanical systems, such as this one at the Mayfield Mall Hewlett-Packard facility, are typical for Geo. H. Wilson, Inc. (1986)

a team of horses pulling a Petaluma Haypress at the early age of 11 on Will Purdy's Swanton Ranch; who marched in San Francisco as a navel reservist during the 1915 World's Fair, dedicated by President Howard Taft; who worked on a steam-powered concrete mixer on Branciforte Avenue, Santa Cruz's first paved street; who was a volunteer fireman during the changeover from horses to combustion engines; who trained many of the people who today have their

Geo. H. Wilson looks on as grandson Tom Wilson inspects the huge fans about to be installed in the University of California, Santa Cruz, library. Photo taken in 1966

own plumbing and heating firms in Santa Cruz; who installed much of the original plumbing in Seabright; and who actively ran a business in town that was built on quality workmanship and service for more than 50 years is still the chairman of the board of Geo. H. Wilson, Inc.

PARTNERS IN PROGRESS

123

CREDIT BUREAU OF SANTA CRUZ COUNTY

During the 1950s the Credit Bureau was located upstairs at 118 Union Street. Later, in the 1960s, the firm occupied the entire building.

The Credit Bureau of Santa Cruz County is probably one of the least understood local businesses. Yet it is also one of the most necessary, not only to its 400 credit-granting members, but also to the thousands of consumers who benefit from its fast, accurate, and updated credit reporting services.

It can be assumed that no one, be they consumer or commercial concern, intentionally creates an unpaid, past due debt. Yet it happens. Thus, someone has to look after collecting such a debt, and that is one of the two core responsibilities assigned to the Credit Bureau of Santa Cruz County by its clients. In order to accomplish this goal, professional collectors attempt to recover all types of delinquent accounts and convert them into cash. The Credit Bureau also strives to maintain an impersonal and professional attitude at all times in conversations and documented comments with debtors. The firm works to retain client and customer goodwill, and all actions are in accordance with federal and state laws, rules, and regulations.

The second responsibility of the Credit Bureau is to provide credit information services. Each month the organization provides more than 20,000 credit reports to its members. This includes everything from bank and finance companies, to retail stores, to service and professional firms that wish to extend credit. The Credit Bureau is serviced by TRW, the largest on-line, computerized credit reporting system in the United States. As a result, its members have direct access to TRW's 144 million consumer and business files via high-speed data communication lines.

Of course, the Credit Bureau of Santa Cruz County wasn't always a source of instantaneous information. Back in 1927, when Stanley Huffman and Jack Enns first started out as Huffman & Enns Credit Adjustors, it was a single desk and chair collection operation. The following year the firm added credit reporting to its services, moved into a new office in the Rittenhouse Building, and changed its name to Central Finance & Adjustment.

In 1932 the company became the Credit Bureau of Santa Cruz when it received qualification as an affiliated member of the Associated Credit Bureaus of America. By the following year the Credit Bureau had grown to 12 employees, with Enns in charge of collections and Huffman handling credit reporting and membership development. Due to a need for more space, the firm moved into larger offices over the Mission Drive-in Market on Front Street, where it remained more than 20 years.

In 1943 Jack Enns left the business. From then on Stanley Huffman ran the credit bureau at various locations until his untimely death in 1967. Since that time his son, John S. Huffman, current president of the Credit Bureau, has continued to run an ever-changing and more complex operation.

Today the Credit Bureau of Santa Cruz County has 42 full-time employees involved in everything from collections to accounts receivable management services for health care people, from credit information to credit counseling services that help people better manage their financial obligations.

In 1985 the Credit Bureau moved into this spacious 8,000-square-foot building that was specially designed to meet the current and future needs of the business.

ALIBERTI CONSTRUCTION INCORPORATED

Down on Swift Street in Santa Cruz is the firm of Aliberti Construction, where you will find Joe Aliberti, his wife, Linda, his son Mike, longtime foreman Jerry Casey, and several other employees continuing to do what they have done so well for the past 35 years. Namely, they construct quality custom homes; they specialize in insurance work such as fire and water damage repair; they build commercial buildings; and they do "anything else that comes along," from a $200 floor repair to a $2-million, 42-unit motel complex. For Joe Aliberti, "the ornery little Italian kid from Davenport," a lot of hard work and relying on his reputation has gotten Aliberti Construction to where it is today.

Joe likes to relate that in 1949, while most of his buddies went off to college, he went to study at "Davenport City College," the local cement plant. Fortunately, he became a carpenter's helper six months after he started. Up until that time Joe hadn't known what he wanted for an occupation, but the helper's job changed all that. "I loved pounding nails," he recalls. For the next six years, with two years out for the Army, Joe continued learning the trade. In 1955 he decided he wanted to be more than a carpenter, and he left the cement plant to join the union. Ironically, he would work for the same contractor, Paul Hirsch, for the next seven years.

By 1962 Joe had become so good at all the aspects of contracting that Hirsch made him a partner, and the firm became Hirsh and Aliberti. In 1972, when Hirsch wanted to move to Oregon, Joe bought him out, and Joe Aliberti Construction came into being. A few years ago, when son Mike joined him, Joe changed the name to Aliberti Construction Incorporated. "It was better that way" says a proud Joe Aliberti, because "some day he'll run it."

Today Aliberti Construction continues to survive in a highly competitive market. "Nobody is going to give you more for your dollar than we do," says Joe. "We build with dependable car-

The current 11,000-square-foot company offices, built by Joe Aliberti in 1975, were constructed to replace an old warehouse out of which Hirsch & Aliberti, and later Joe Aliberti Construction, operated for many years.

Joe Aliberti stands in front of his original office, a garage at his former residence in Santa Cruz, from which he started Aliberti Construction Incorporated.

penters and craftsmen who have worked for us for years, and we're willing to sacrifice a little profit to make the job a little nicer." Currently Joe Aliberti manages the company and does the estimating. Son Mike does all of the necessary drafting, supervises crews on site, and is the general superintendent. Joe's wife, Linda, oversees the office management and staff, and also has her own carpet and drape business, which operates out of the same location.

Although much more could be said about Aliberti Construction Incorporated, suffice it to say the firm has done quality work for many local individuals and businesses, at reasonable prices, at literally thousands of locations all over Santa Cruz County and the Monterey Bay area. Perhaps the best example of the company being one of the many Santa Cruz County Partners In Progress is the office bulletin board, which is covered with many letters of appreciation from satisfied customers for jobs well done. Originally Joe Aliberti put it up so his employees could get some positive feedback on the good work that they had accomplished. However, after several years, it also seems to have become a source of pride—the local kid from Davenport makes good!

SANTA CRUZ COUNTY

WATSONVILLE AREA CHAMBER OF COMMERCE & AGRICULTURE

One of the things that makes Santa Cruz County such a Restless Paradise is the diversity of individual community needs encountered in the very different localities within the area. In the north county, most needs are related to open space, forested mountain land, and state parks. In the mid-county, where it is primarily residential and commercial in nature, needs revolve around business and social services. And in the south county, a majority of the community finds its needs associated with agriculture and development.

For the past 67 years the Watsonville

Kids and apple trees—Watsonville, a great place to grow.

At the 23rd annual Watsonville Antique Fly-In, a Ryan PT-22 taxis out to perform in the air show.

Area Chamber of Commerce & Agriculture has successfully addressed those needs in the south county. Today, because most of its 700 members are in agribusiness, the needs of that industry are a primary part of the chamber's program. Similarly, unlike other areas of the county, the Watsonville area still has much land, housing, and industry to be developed. As a result, the chamber spends a considerable amount of time supporting local economic growth and development. Currently the organization has no less than 13 separate ongoing committees, with more than 700 involved members actively dealing with many community issues, both business and residential.

To quote the present chamber manager, Charlene Shaffer, "The chamber's mission has always been to make the Watsonville area a better place to work, play, and do business profitably." Back in 1920, when the organization was first founded as the Pajaro Valley Chamber of Commerce, the then-*Evening Pajaronian* of February 28 reported: "the organization . . .will go in for civic improvement, community entertainment and amusements, the beautifying of town and country, and other projects to develop the district into a live, progressive, up-to-date, public-spirited community."

According to local Watsonville historian Betty Lewis, activities in which the chamber was involved in its first year included, "a day nursery, Community Christmas Tree and Festival, orphan's dinner, plus the mailing of pamphlets and literature extolling the progressive and enlightened outlook of the Pajaro Valley Chamber of Commerce." From these historic beginnings the organization has continued basically unchanged up to the present day, representing the interests of a small town in a rural farming community—a small town, however, with a big eye to the future.

Back in 1928 several far-thinking local residents got the idea that if Watsonville had an airport, that would certainly put the area on the map. On May 9, 1931, through the efforts of an active chamber, the three-runway Watsonville Municipal Airport was officially opened. Today, some 56 years later, the Antique Fly-In Air Show, sponsored by the chamber, uses that exact same airport for one of the largest such shows in the western United States. Every Memorial Day weekend for the past 23 years, 350 antique aircraft have flown into Watsonville to perform before thousands of spectators. For the Watsonville area, this is the major fund-raising event of the year. Suffice it to say that because of the hard work and effort put forth by the Watsonville Area Chamber of Commerce & Agriculture every year to make this and other events a success, the Pajaro Valley/Watsonville area is definitely on the map.

DOMINICAN SANTA CRUZ HOSPITAL

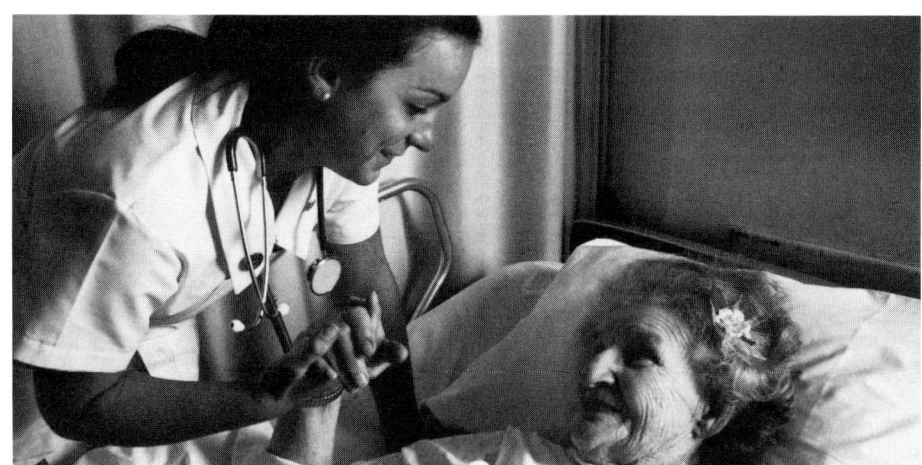

Throughout its history Dominican has been known for the personal touch of its staff.

In 1941, responding to a request by the Santa Cruz Catholic community, the Bishop of Monterey asked the Dominican Sisters of Adrian, Michigan, to start a hospital in the Catholic health care tradition. The Sisters purchased the unoccupied, 28-bed Hanly Hospital on West Cliff Drive, refurbished it, and renamed it Sisters Hospital.

Motivated by the enthusiastic response of the community to their dedication, compassion, and high-quality care, the Adrian Sisters—with the community's help—purchased Santa Cruz Hospital on Soquel Avenue in 1951 and added "Dominican" to its name. The Sisters operated both hospitals until 1967, when the present Dominican Santa Cruz Hospital facility opened.

Santa Cruz' need in the mid-1960s for a large, modern hospital was apparent from rapid growth of the area and the advances in medical science. The Sisters, helped by a generous outpouring of time and effort from community volunteers, launched a fund-raising drive that was enthusiastically responded to by the public. They purchased a 17-acre site on Soquel Drive, which provided room for future expansion; by the end of 1967 the new Dominican Santa Cruz Hospital was dedicated.

Today the original hospital building is surrounded by many others, including office buildings occupied by physicians of nearly every medical specialty. In the ensuing years Dominican has kept its pledge to provide health care services locally whenever feasible. During the 1970s the hospital expanded, adding the Business and Administration Office building and a new wing that housed a larger laboratory, the Medical Records Department, the Cardiopulmonary Department, Physical Medicine (occupational and physical therapy, and communications disorders), more diagnostic imaging services, and conference rooms.

Throughout its history Dominican has provided the most up-to-date proven medical technology for the people of Santa Cruz. The hospital has been the leader on the Central Coast in diagnostic and surgical technology, such as magnetic resonance imaging (MRI), CAT scanning, and laser and outpatient surgery.

As the 1980s approached, Dominican continued to expand to meet growing needs. Another successful fund drive helped finance a three-part expansion. The first phase was the completion in 1983 of the 28-bed inpatient Mental Health Unit, the only such facility in Santa Cruz County, and the Education Center, home of the community education program called PEP, the Personal Enrichment Program. Phase two concluded with the dedication in July 1984 of the North Wing, housing a new skilled nursing unit, enlarged Critical Care and Outpatient Surgery units, and offices of support personnel.

In phase three, completed in 1985, the original hospital building was remodeled, including the development of the Adrian Center, an alcohol and drug dependency treatment program; the Women's Diagnostic Center for mammography; the Outpatient Oncology Unit; and enlargement of the Family Birthing Center.

Plans for additional programs are still under way at Dominican Santa Cruz Hospital as it continues to be a dynamic, innovative institution, combining the best of modern science and scrupulous professionalism with the traditions of the Catholic health care ministry carried on by the Adrian Dominican Sisters: their commitment to providing quality health care and their belief that true healing involves the totality of a human being—the spiritual, emotional, and the social, as well as the physical.

Adrian Dominican Sisters near the entrance of the hospital, shortly after the present facility was completed in 1967.

PLANTRONICS, INC.

It is almost impossible to turn on a television set anywhere in the world and not see the primary product that Plantronics of Santa Cruz manufactures—namely, corded and cordless, headband and headband-free headsets and related telephones. Plantronics currently produces 75 percent of all such headsets used in the United States and a major portion of those used in Europe. Its customers include AT&T, the Federal Aviation Administration, reservation clerks in all fields, the many deregulated Bell systems, airline pilots, NASA astronauts, stockbrokers, medical personnel, and corporate telephone operators. In terms of scope and size, this breaks down to a 1,200-employee, Santa Cruz-headquartered, $100-million-plus-per-year communications corporation.

Of course it wasn't always this way for the first electronics high-tech firm established in Santa Cruz County. Back in May 1961 two friends, Courtney Graham and Keith Larkin, decided to go into business together, producing either aircraft accessories or golf aids. The reason for their indecision was because Graham was a copilot for United Airlines and Larkin ran a flying service, yet they were both avid golfers. They both had a lot of ideas, but

Neil J. Hynes, president and chief executive officer of Plantronics, Inc.

nothing specific. To get started, however, they finally incorporated under the name of Plane Aids. That name was changed to Pacific Plantronics, which ultimately became Plantronics.

They began the process of raising money by importing and selling a Japanese

The new corporate offices of Plantronics, Inc., in Santa Cruz.

product—radio spectacle sunglasses that had a built-in miniature radio and a small ear plug. As Graham traveled around the country for United Air Lines, he was able to sell about 1,500 of the units. Ironically, the glasses ended up in a United Airlines employee store where the chief pilot saw them. He went to Graham and Larkin and told them that if a kind of light headset, similar to what was found in the glasses, could be made available to pilots, they might buy them. Larkin, the inventor of the two, told him he and his partner were already working on it. Two weeks later Larkin returned with a balsa wood mock-up. United Airlines was excited about the idea, and development began in earnest.

Needing financial backing for development costs, Graham one day replaced all the reading material in the seat backs aboard a United cross-country charter flight of top executives with his company's prospectus. Unbelievably someone bit, and the partners got their backing.

In 1962 Pacific Plantronics got its start in a portion of the West Mushroom plant, now O.T. Price's, in Soquel. West had become an investor and had offered Graham and Larkin a place to begin their business. The first year, with four part-time employees—including Courtney's neighbor, engineer Don Wilson who is still with the firm—Pacific Plantronics managed to sell about $15,000 in product.

In June 1962 they approached the FAA, NASA, and Bell Laboratories. Bell said they were not interested, and the FAA showed some interest; however, NASA bought them for the Mercury Eleven launch. This one vote of confidence put Plantronics on track.

The following year Western Electric ordered 17,000 headsets for Pacific Bell. The sale demonstrated that there was a real demand for lightweight, comfortable headsets using miniature microphones and receivers and transistorized circuitry.

In 1965 Larkin left Plantronics to pursue other interests. At that point Graham assumed the presidency of the company. Shortly thereafter, Plantronics received nationwide acceptance by AT&T of their MS-50 lightweight headset, and the rest is history. Almost immediately Graham brought in new manufacturing and production people. The firm took over a 1,200-square-foot building at 111 Josephine; subsequently, the facility was expanded to 8,800 square feet.

In 1967 the company discovered that just about the time it started doing business with Bell, Bell began developing its own version of the Plantronics' unit. By 1968 Bell was arranging for the manufacture of its own product. It was at this point that Graham decided that if the corporation was to stay in business it was not only going to have to compete, it was going to have to produce a better product.

According to Bob Bernardi, one of the three engineers on the development team, Courtney set down the following specifications: "It had to be better—extremely lightweight, comfortable, no headband, and something you could pop in your ear like a peanut and turn out like bottle caps." Two months later the StarSet® was born. It weighed in at 11 grams, was hands and headband free, and offered a four-to-one reduction in background noise when the user was not talking.

The StarSet® was previewed to AT&T in 1969, on the market by January 1970, sold to Bell in April 1971, and had displaced the Bell Laboratories unit and become the Bell System standard by 1973.

The following year Plantronics consolidated all its Santa Cruz facilities into one large building that used to house the Sylvania plant. Since then the firm has continued to expand at that location. It also has acquired several smaller communications companies along the way, including Frederick Electronics Corporation in Maryland; Kentrox Industries, Inc., in Portland, Oregon; Wilcom Products, Inc., in New Hampshire; and Walker Communications in Georgia. Altogether there are five manufacturing facilities in the United States and a subassembly plant in Mexico.

As Plantronics entered the 1980s, it had seen both good and bad times. With the advent of the Walkman concept, the headband headset saw a resurgence in demand. As a result, the company developed the Supra model. Within two years it represented half of the firm's sales volume. From 1982 to 1984 Plantronics' patents on its headsets ran out, and the firm began to see some stiff competition. In addition, the Bell system monopoly was split, scattering its customer base. As a result, the firm had to go back through distribution and reestablish its customers.

Today Plantronics continues to grow and develop new products. Courtney Graham stepped down almost 10 years ago, and Neil J. Hynes is now the firm's president and chief executive officer. His skills are leading the way for a company that has found its niche in producing communications equipment that focuses on the human interface.

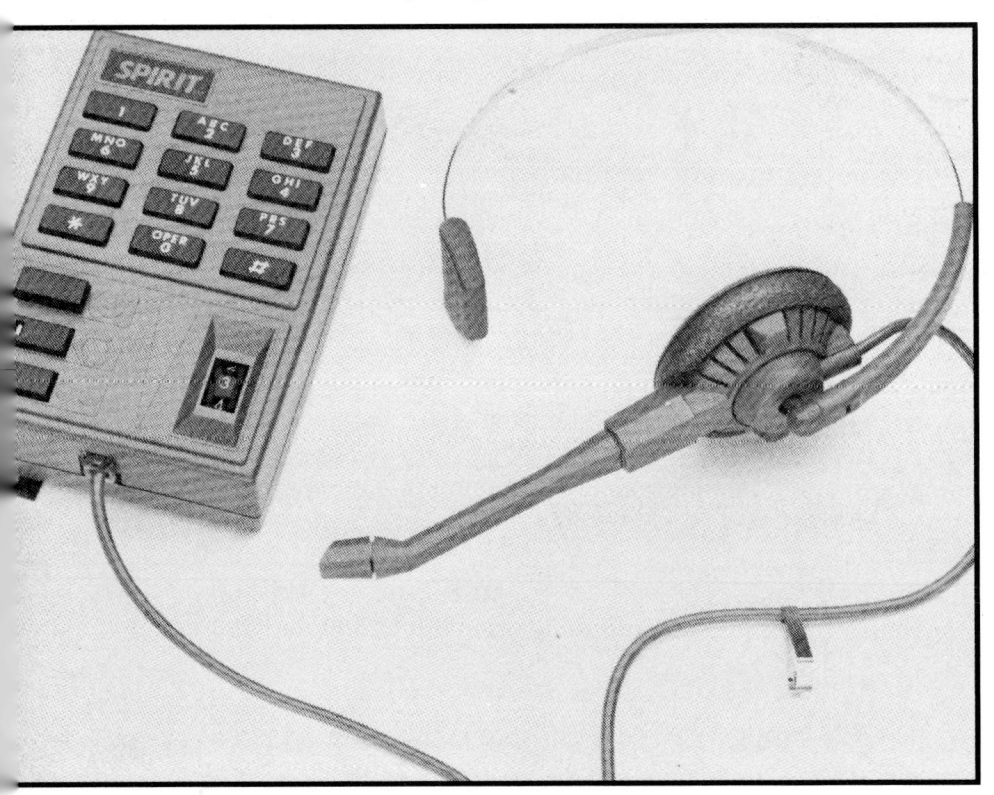

Typical of Plantronics' product line is the new "Spirit 4" headset telephone for hand-free consumer communications.

PENNIMAN TITLE COMPANY

When H.W.H. Penniman and his wife, Leonora, first came to Santa Cruz shortly before 1910, Penniman began a photographic supply business with Jack Converse. Their company, known as C&P, had its offices downstairs in the Moore Building next to the United Cigar Store. Although interested in photography, Penniman was also a licensed surveyor and had worked for various title companies. In 1914, recognizing a need in Santa Cruz County, he left the photographic business and started the sole proprietorship of H.W.H. Penniman, Searcher of Records, at One Locust Street in downtown Santa Cruz. His services, with the help of one part-time employee, included notary public, abstractor, and conveyancer.

By 1925 the business had prospered to such an extent that expansion had taken place in the old Locust Street bank building, and the firm was operating under a new name, which it retains to this day, Penniman Santa Cruz County Title Company.

H.W.H. Penniman was a man of many skills and was well liked and trusted throughout the county. Among other things, he was responsible for laying out Brookdale and much of Scotts Valley. In addition to his varied abilities, Penniman was also well known just by his stature. At only five feet tall, he was a small man. Grandson Ed says, "He weighed in at birth at just one pound. His first crib was a shoe box...What a great legacy he left us all."

H.W.H. Penniman passed away in 1935. The company he left behind, which had grown to the point of requiring 16 full-time employees, was reorganized into a partnership consisting of his widow, Leonora, and his sons, George, Warren, and John.

It was about this time that a change in the title business occurred nationwide. Prior to that time when someone bought or sold property they went to an abstractor who would bring the abstract up to date. An abstract was simply a continuing record showing all that had previously occurred with that property via private and public record search. Once an abstract was current, a lawyer would write an opinion as to whether the property was merchantable. If the buyer and seller concurred, the deal was consummated. Later, rather than directly involving the abstract, a certificate of title was issued that simply noted any changes in the abstract, kept at the title insurance company, since the previous transfer of ownership. In the 1930s title insurance began to be issued guaranteeing the seller of the title that if there was an error on the part of the insurance company, the insurance company would bear the burden of rectifying the error.

In 1936 Penniman Title contracted with Fidelity Title Insurance Company of Sacramento to be its underwriter. Although Fidelity subsequently became part of Safeco—which is now wholly owned by Chicago Title Insurance Company, the largest such company in the United States—it still underwrites Penniman Title and has for 51 years.

In 1940 Penniman Title Company became a California corporation. Today Penniman Title Company remains an independent title company with Warren Penniman and his son, Warren Penniman, Jr., actively representing the concerns of the company. With H.W.H.'s great-grandson David Penniman now working for the firm, Penniman Title is into its fourth generation in Santa Cruz County. To quote Warren Sr., "We still do the job thoroughly, the right way, and we don't take any shortcuts." With 55 employees and offices in Felton, Aptos, Watsonville, and Santa Cruz, Penniman Title continues as a strong Partner in Progress.

Small in stature yet tall in ability, H.W.H. Penniman founded the company in 1914 and provided services as a notary public, abstractor, and conveyancer.

WILSON BROTHERS & ASSOCIATES, INC.

When you ask 40-year-plus sales and appraisal veteran Tanner Wilson of Wilson Brothers & Associates, Inc., the oldest real estate firm in Santa Cruz County, how long the company has been around, he usually responds, "Well, we're not strangers in town." That is an understatement.

The foundation for Wilson Brothers started with David Wilson in the 1870s and was helped along by two exceptional Wilson women of the time. The first, Martha Wilkington Wilson, a widow who lost her husband and two of her three children to diphtheria in 1862, came west with son David to Santa Cruz from Illinois in 1871. Possessing a strong business sense, she soon made several substantial Santa Cruz property investments and profitable transactions. The second woman was Emma Goodspeed Wilson, who came from a family with excellent skills in finance and merchandising and was the smart young wife of David. Together Martha and Emma were the driving force behind much of David Wilson's early success.

Although David Wilson would go on over the next 40 years to make millions of dollars in different business dealings, it wouldn't be with Emma. In 1899 he left his wife and five children and moved to Washington State. Undaunted, Emma founded the Emma Goodspeed Wilson Investment and Improvement Company that same year. Thus began the Wilson real estate empire.

In 1910 Frank and David Jr., two of Emma's four sons, went on to form Wilson Brothers & Associates, Inc. The firm's centrally located headquarters was at 140 Pacific Avenue, and the business came complete with two four-passenger automobiles and a telephone.

The business flourished until the Depression, when things were tough. A new house could be built for $3,500. Lots on paved streets sold for under $500. Buildings on Pacific Avenue rented for 10 cents per square foot. Twenty-five thousand dollars would buy a 200-acre mountain apple ranch with home and outbuildings. A reasonably good home sold for $2,000 and land went for $10 an acre. Lots at tax sale were auctioned at $1.18. The now-popular "Victorian" was a drag on the market—who would want the big old house with all those stained-glass windows? They were neglected and torn down.

Tanner G. Wilson

Things were looking brighter by the time Tanner Wilson joined his father and uncle in the business after graduating from Stanford in 1938.

Tanner successfully sold and developed real estate in Santa Cruz for four decades. In May 1982 Wilson Brothers was sold to his son, David L. Wilson, who today represents the fourth generation of the Wilson family to sell real estate in Santa Cruz. Among the many changes David has instituted are separate and expanded residential and commercial departments. Also an Appraisal Corporation has been formed with Edward "Bud" Prindle M.A.I. as president with more than 30 years' experience.

Although things have changed considerably over the years, competent and expert help are still Wilson Brothers' trademarks. With 25 salespeople and employees, Wilson Brothers remains an active part of the Santa Cruz community. Wilson Brothers has carried on a tradition of integrity and service, and a reputation it guards jealously and intends to keep.

The Wilson brothers, circa 1910, are (from left) Frank, Jay, David, and Charles.

RITTENHOUSE INSURANCE CENTER

Three generations of the Rittenhouse family today stand behind the Insurance Center. In back row are (from left) Bob Sr. and Robert R. III, in the middle Ryan F. and Bob Jr., and in the very front is Ivan F. Rittenhouse.

It was 1902 when a young Emmet Cloyd Rittenhouse, originally from Ohio, came to California to die. He had served in the Spanish American War and had contracted yellow fever. With proper care and perhaps somewhat due to Santa Cruz' salubrious weather, he recovered.

Rittenhouse settled in Santa Cruz where he started the Busy Bee barber shop. With good health and blessed with an ambitious nature, he was able to use his earnings to pay his way through Stanford University. He later graduated from law school and returned to Santa Cruz, where he practiced law for many years out of an old theater. The theater was converted into stores and offices, and in time became known as the Rittenhouse Building.

Always conscious of his deep family ties, Rittenhouse brought his next oldest brother out from Ohio to serve an apprenticeship in the barber shop and go to school. In this manner brothers Oscar Floyd, Arthur Royde, Martin Loyde, and Ross Ray Rittenhouse all arrived in California, began a trade at the Busy Bee, and went on to school.

In later years Arthur worked for Shell Oil and joined his brother Oscar in a business partnership that became the Rittenhouse Clothing Store. Martin went on to raise mushrooms and bullfrogs, and Ross went into the insurance business. Hoping to keep the family together, the five brothers brought their father, mother, and two sisters out to California. Once here, the family purchased a small farm on Thurber Lane and Soquel Drive, which they worked for a number of years.

In 1930 Ross began his independent insurance agency in a back office of the Rittenhouse Building, and after several years was able to hire his first secretary. Because times were hard during the Depression years and the buying of insurance was not a priority, it took many long hours and hard work to survive. Still, in all, Santa Cruz was a good community, and the spirit was to support your own local citizen. Eventually things turned around, and the firm prospered. By the end of World War II Ross was selling about $32,000 per year in policies, and he was able to support his family from the commissions earned.

During that time the relationship between the insurance company and the independent agent was almost a partnership. Companies would typically pay for an agent's stationery and his long-distance telephone calls. They would also add incentives by taking agents out to dinner while hoping to receive more business. In addition, service people were always in the field willing to help. In those days an agent's

For years Bob Rittenhouse, Sr., has had a preoccupation with fire engines and firehouse memorabilia. The Insurance Center, besides selling insurance, is a firehouse museum in disuse.

word was sufficient, and a handshake was a deal. Clients could make arrangements over the phone on a gentleman's agreement, and lawsuits and lawyers were almost unheard of. However, as time went on, insurance companies became bigger and corporate decisions prevailed. The agent took more of an adversary position to continue doing a professional job for his client.

After working for two years at the Union Ice Company on Chestnut Street, Robert (Bob Ross' son) attended San Jose State and in 1946 married Edithann Gates.

Bob returned to Santa Cruz and started his own life insurance agency. Several years later Ross became grand master of the Independent Order of Odd Fellows for the state of California. Because Ross had to travel extensively as grand master, Bob joined his father and they hired their first secretary.

Following Ross' death in 1950, Bob Rittenhouse found himself alone in the insurance business that his father had founded. He skillfully picked up where his father left off and successfully continued on for the next 10 years.

In 1960 Bob Rittenhouse joined with Jim Thomas and Jim Fearnehough to form the Insurance Center. With the three pooling their skills, resources, and clients, larger offices were required. As a result, the company was moved to the east side of Santa Cruz on Soquel Avenue, where it remained for some time.

Tragedy struck just one year later when Jim Fearnehough died suddenly. In January 1963 Dave Sachau joined Rittenhouse and Thomas.

Sachau was held in high esteem by all, and was known as a renowned sportsman who loved to fish the San Lorenzo River. Tragedy struck a second time as one year later David died suddenly.

About the same time Doug Austin and Bill Moore joined Rittenhouse and Thomas, and the firm had some of its finest years. Thomas retired, and Austin and Moore started their own agencies. As the community grew so did the Insurance Center—into the 1980s.

Today the Rittenhouse Insurance Center continues as an independent broker/agency. Being an independent allows it to shop among the many companies who service the firm so employees can write the best policy to suit their individual client's needs. Likewise, because the Rittenhouse Insurance Center can write policies for many companies, it can offer a wide variety of insurance from home owners' and auto, and from very large businesses and industries. Bonds became one of its fortes.

The Rittenhouse Insurance Center remains a family business. Currently Robert Rittenhouse, Sr., is president. His son, Robert Jr., has looked after the many day-to-day problems for several years. Unlike the days of Ross Rittenhouse, it now takes a staff of 16 people to look after the insurance needs of Santa Cruz County. The company could have grown larger and expanded into other communities;

The Rittenhouse family members (top row, left to right) are Oscar Floyd, Martin Loyde, Emmet Cloyd. In the bottom row (left to right) are Ross Ray; Rubin B., father of the five brothers; and Arthur Royde. Photo circa 1918

however, it chose to stay local. As a result, many of Ross Rittenhouse's former clients remain with the firm. Ironically, the Rittenhouse Insurance Center is back downtown, still in the Rittenhouse Building, next door to where the business got its start. As to the future, the firm will continue to be a family-run operation. With Robert R., son of Robert Jr., now working for the company on a part-time basis, a fourth generation has entered the business.

The Rittenhouse family has not only served Santa Cruz County with insurance needs, but also as an active participant in community affairs and organizations. Both Bob Sr. and Jr. are active members in the International Order of Odd Fellows, having held many offices. Bob Sr. has served on the Planning Commission and the Water Commission, as past district chairman of the Boy Scouts, and as president of the Insurance Agents Association.

BED & BREAKFAST INNKEEPERS OF SANTA CRUZ COUNTY

With all the natural and man-made attractions that Santa Cruz County has to offer the six million people who live within 50 miles of its borders, as well as the many others who visit the area, it is a natural for tourism. As a result, many forms of accommodations are necessary to meet the diverse requirements of those who choose to visit the area. One mode of accommodation that has recently found a genuine rebirth and a renewed success within the county is the bed and breakfast inn, patterned after those found earlier in this country's history and throughout Europe.

Currently the Bed & Breakfast Innkeepers of Santa Cruz County offer nine such establishments that allow their many customers the chance to relax and momentarily drift back in time to perhaps a more carefree, charming period of opulence and elegance.

The Chateau Victorian, typical of the many 1900s Santa Cruz Victorians that have lovingly been restored to their original style and grace, is a two-story structure situated one block from the beach and boardwalk. Each of the seven guest rooms has been individually decorated to reflect Victorian period color and decor. Found in the rooms are amenities such as genuine hand-painted and sketched art of the time, various styles of fireplaces, peaked and open-beam ceilings, antique furniture, a claw-foot bathtub, secluded wooden decks, and a private patio. Legend has it that the friendly ghost of the sea captain who originally built the house wanders the halls from time to time to the delight of all concerned.

The Babbling Brook Inn, situated just off Highway 1 in Santa Cruz, is located on Laurel Creek. There pine and redwood trees, cascading waterfalls, and a meandering stream grace an acre of gardens, private decks, patios, a gazebo, and a covered footbridge. The inn, built in 1909 on the foundations of an 1870s tannery and a 1790s gristmill, is the oldest and largest bed and breakfast inn in the Santa Cruz area. Twelve beautiful rooms, decorated in a country French decor, await the visitor. Previously a well-known French restaurant, the Babbling Brook Inn has been redone to reflect the same ambience.

The Apple Lane Inn of Aptos is truly a historic as well as a Victorian gem. The house was originally built in 1876 by Benjamin and George Porter on a 60-acre parcel of apple orchards and grazing land. In 1966 the house and its 2.5 acres were purchased after standing empty for 30 years. The next 19 years were spent patiently reconstructing, restoring, and preserving the structure. In 1981 it opened as the Apple Lane Inn and has remained in operation since then. The rustic charm of the five guest rooms, coupled with the Victorian parlor, library, sitting room, cider room, and brick patio sheltered by its many hanging plants, makes the Apple Lane Inn a perfect place to get away from it all.

Chateau des Fleurs is an elegant early mansion built in 1879 in the mountain community of Ben Lomond, near the pristine San Lorenzo River. At the time of its construction the area, then known as Pacific Mills, was a prime lumber shipping point on the great valley lumber flume. Located in a choice mountain setting on Highway 9, among oak, madrona, pine, and redwood trees, this historic home was once owned by the Bartlett family of pear fame. Offering three spacious guest rooms, a large gallery, a library, and a very different atmosphere, complete with antique wood stoves and forest scenery, the Chateau des Fleurs is definitely a step back in time.

The Mangels' House, built in the 1880s, was the Aptos country home of Claus Mangels, who, together with his brother-in-law Claus Spreckels, founded the sugar beet industry in California. The house remained in the same family until 1979, when it came to the new owners with nostalgic reminiscences of vacations spent there a half-century ago. Situated on four acres of lawn, orchard, and woodland, the Mangels' House is an ideal retreat from the city. Complete with sitting and guest rooms and five beautifully decorated guest bedrooms, it offers British hospitality in the old style. Close to the 10,000-acre Forest of Niscene Marks and Monterey Bay, the Mangels' House is a natural getaway.

The New Davenport Bed & Breakfast Inn, nine miles up the coast from Santa Cruz, is a composite of both the old and the new. Four of the guest bedrooms are located in the oldest building in Davenport. Originally a public bathhouse and then a bar, restaurant, and dance hall, the building was later converted into a private residence. More recently it was renovated and is now a part of the inn. The other eight guest bedrooms are situated above the new Cash Store and Restaurant—a recent structure built in 1978 in the tradition of the original store that occupied the same corner for so many years. Tastefully decorated and furnished in a mixture of antiques, ethnic treasures, and local arts and crafts, most of the rooms overlook the scenic Pacific Ocean from high on the bluff at Davenport.

The Darling House is a 1910 oceanside mansion designed by famed California architect, William Weeks, for William Seward Iliff, Colorado cattle baron and founder of Denver University Graduate School and Iliff School of Theology. Stunning hardwood inlays, beveled glass, and blazing open hearths are complemented with Tiffanys, Chippendales, and other nineteenth-century antiques in every room. Spacious lawns, colorful gardens, and spectacular ocean views from seven of the eight guest rooms create an atmosphere of peaceful elegance. Stroll to the lighthouse, boardwalk, secluded beaches, romantic restaurants on the wharf; sail or surf; or simply relax into another century in the hand-crocheted hammock beneath the glorious hanging begonias on the sweeping oceanside veranda to the seranade of seals and pounding surf.

Fairview Manor, residing on three acres of secluded land along the beautiful San Lorenzo River, nestled deep in the heart of the Santa Cruz Mountains, is a romantic getaway. Constructed in 1924 on the site of the old Ben Lomond Hotel for prominent San Francisco patent attorney N.A. Acker and his family, Fairview

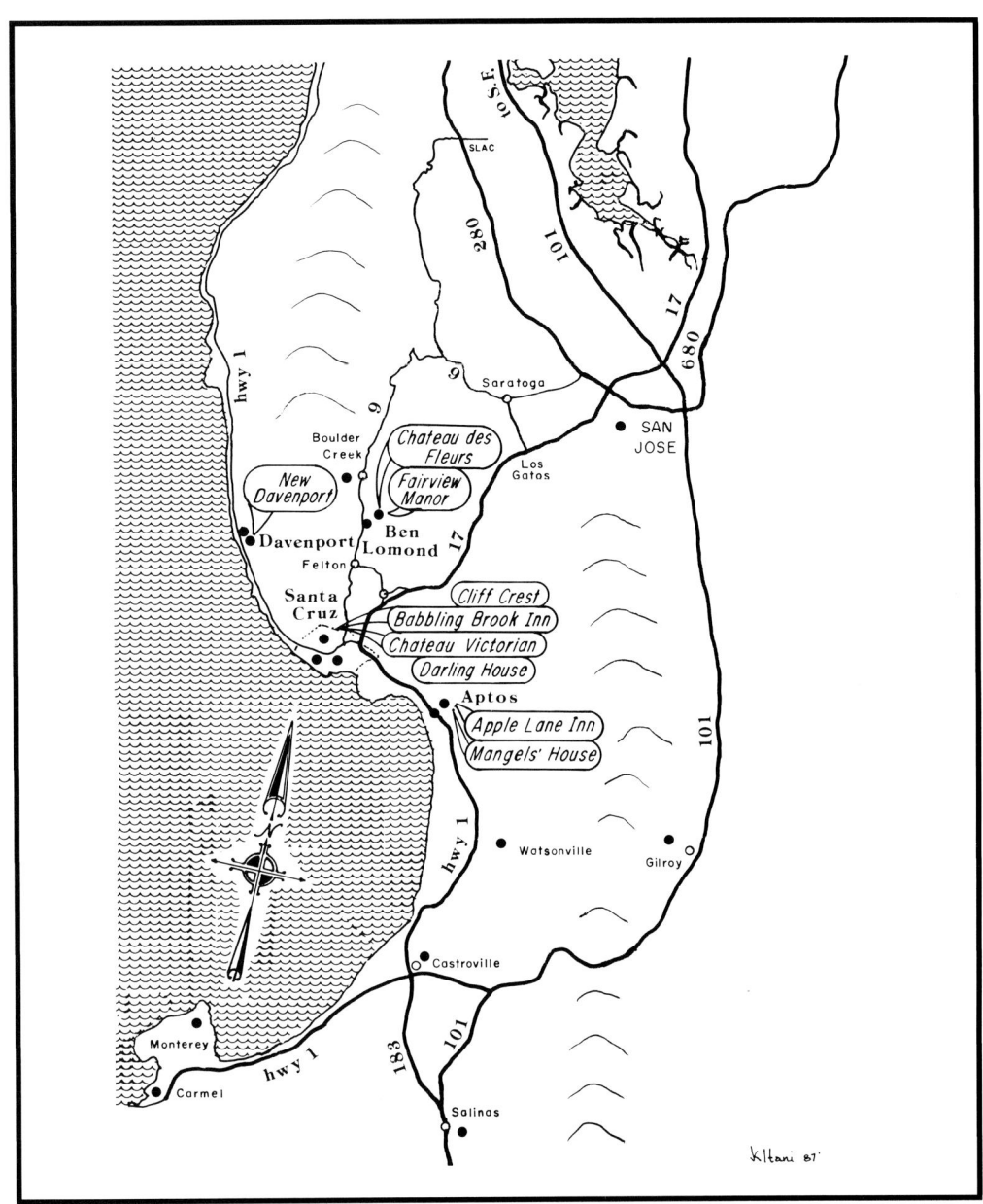

The nine Bed & Breakfast Inns shown here have easy access from any direction in California.

Manor served for many years as a summer residence. The home was maintained by the family until 1981, when the present owners acquired the property. The beautifully landscaped grounds, with its winding pathways leading to charming, restful areas on the river or by the lovely fish pond, together with the five unique guest rooms and spacious living room with its majestic stone fireplace, exhibit the warmth and comfort found only during an earlier, quieter time.

Cliff Crest is a perfect example of a time when romantic ambience and the comforting pleasures of home were enjoyed at a pleasant, unhurried pace. A classic Queen Anne Victorian mansion, situated on Beach Hill in Santa Cruz overlooking Monterey Bay, the home was originally built in 1887 for William Jeter. Jeter, at one time lieutenant governor of California, was one of the early ecologists responsible for the establishment of the California Redwood State Park, Big Basin. The lush grounds and spacious gardens of the estate were designed by Jeter's friend John McLaren, most famous for his design of San Francisco's Golden Gate Park. This historic setting, coupled with Cliff Crest's five unique guest rooms, parlor, and solarium, provide the perfect atmosphere for peace, quiet friendship, and a sense of romance.

As can be expected, all of the inns offer various breakfast enticements as well as the extra amenities and services found only in such places. All in all, the nine inns of the various Bed & Breakfast Innkeepers of Santa Cruz County are there for anyone who wants a change of pace.

CHAMINADE AT SANTA CRUZ

Unlike any other business in Santa Cruz County, Chaminade at Santa Cruz exists solely to create an environment that is conducive to stimulating learning and informational interchange, both indoors and outdoors, in both structured and casual situations. It has been formulated to be the best executive conference center possible. This is accomplished by taking the individual and group out of the usual stressful day-to-day environment and offering them a place where undisturbed concentration can be accomplished, while at the same time offering visitors complete facilities that look after their total social and physical well-being.

Chaminade, having only been open for business since May 1985, is by far the youngest Partner in Progress represented in this chapter. Yet it, too, has a story to tell. Its primary role is as a place where continuing education has been, and will continue to be, best accomplished. Its architectural tone and subliminal mood reflects the California mission environment, similar to the original one in Santa Cruz. Its philosophical ideals and historical foundation can be traced back almost 200 years. Quoting from the *Chaminade Story*:

Chaminade takes its name from a French priest and educator, Father William Joseph Chaminade. Father Chaminade founded the Society of Mary (Marianists) in the late 1700s with the goal of creating a superior educational system following the chaos of the French Revolution. His efforts produced excellent schools throughout France and then throughout the world. In 1929 Marianist Brothers, a teaching order of the Roman Catholic Church, began construction of the Chaminade boys' high school in Santa Cruz. The building was completed and classes began in 1930...Chaminade functioned as a school until World War II and then became a novitiate utilized to train novices in the Marianist Order. This training facility function continued until the early 1970s, when Chaminade became a religious retreat site.

It was during this period that the

Secluded in a redwood, pine, and eucalyptus forest is Chaminade of Santa Cruz.

At dusk Chaminade offers a breathtaking view of Santa Cruz County and Monterey Bay.

PARTNERS IN PROGRESS

Marianists decided the Santa Cruz property was no longer needed. Used infrequently, it was put up for sale. It was also during this period that three friends began seeing the need for just such a place as Chaminade.

Frank Hildreth, director of the Stanford Sierra Lodge at Fallen Leaf near Lake Tahoe for many years; Larry Swanson, business manager for student housing at U.C. Davis; and Carl Taylor, the manager of a food distribution service that served both places, saw their abilities melding together into one idea. The business community in the San Francisco Bay Area needed a nearby, relaxing, secluded place that was well suited to the learning process, where executives and others could come for a brief stay, year round, and conduct various meetings and seminars. Driven by that idea, the three spent eight months in 1977 looking for just such a place. They found Chaminade at Santa Cruz, and Chaminade found them. In November of that year they acquired the property.

Having an idea is one thing, bringing it to fruition is quite another. It took Hildreth, Swanson, and Taylor more than four years to develop the necessary financing to change an ex-high school into an executive conference center. During that four-year period they faced an almost insurmountable set of problems in order to comply with all the necessary governmental regulations. However, comply they did. New construction and the remodeling of an existing structure began in 1984, with Chaminade at Santa Cruz opening its doors 15 months later.

To meet the requirements of a true corporate campus and continuing education center, Chaminade has paid strict attention to detail. There are 10 fully equipped meeting rooms accommodating from 10 to 300 people. Each meeting room can be connected in any configuration by closed-circuit television, and all rooms boast complete audiovisual systems and computer hookups. The design of each room involves furnishings and decor commensurate with classroom participation, yet comfortable in the style and amenities expected by executives who plan to spend many working hours in the interchange of ideas and technologies.

To enhance the flow of information, Chaminade has installed the latest in audiovisual technology. Video capabilities include broadcast quality, multicamera recording of meetings, multiscreen video playback, and slide and 16-millimeter projectors. Two meeting rooms come with rear-screen projection systems. Audio capabilities include public address systems, and cassette and reel-to-reel recording and playback.

For those whose 152 meetings are scheduled for more than one day, Chaminade provides 152 luxurious guest rooms including 12 spacious suites. Each room affords its guest a study area with two telephones, one of which is available for computer hookup. In addition, guests can request video playback of prerecorded material from the control center. On those days when accommodations are not prebooked for meetings, the rooms are available by reservation for guests wishing just to take advantage of the Chaminade environment.

In the Sunset Dining Room, guests and groups can sit individually or together for a working meal. It is also becoming well known locally for its fine Friday-night seafood buffet and its Sunday brunch. There is also the elegance and intimacy of The Library, where fixed-price, gourmet-menu, six-course dinners are served to 50 people at a time. In addition to the restaurants, there is also a full-service lounge/bar with entertainment provided three to four nights per week.

Chaminade maintains a health club for guests that offers men's and women's steamroom, sauna, and spas. Coeducational facilities include a half-court basketball area, weight rooms, game room, and sports store. Outdoor facilities include four lighted tennis courts, three large spas, sports field, par course, jogging trail, and spacious heated pool. In addition, there are several nature trails wandering in and around Chaminade's

Typical of the quality facilities provided by Chaminade is this meeting room in the main building.

undisturbed forest.

A real understanding of Chaminade of Santa Cruz can only be obtained by visiting it in person. It is not a hotel, nor is it a convention center. It is, however, a place where, individually or collectively, people can expand their horizons. It is the best place in Santa Cruz County, if not California, for effective communication and continuing education at both the corporate and individual level to take place. To quote founding partner Frank Hildreth, "We kept the name 'Chaminade' because it was synonymous with 'learning.'"

CABRILLO COLLEGE

Perhaps one of the most important Partners in Progress for Santa Cruz County and other nearby areas is Cabrillo College in Aptos. Founded in 1959, Cabrillo College is a public community college offering area residents quality instruction by an outstanding faculty. Classes provide preparation for transfer to a four-year university, training in a variety of occupational programs, and many opportunities for personal enrichment and professional development. Daytime and evening classes are offered on the Aptos campus and on off-campus sites in Felton, Scotts Valley, and Watsonville. The new Cabrillo College Center in Watsonville reflects a commitment to easy access to the college's programs, and it underscores the college's long-standing close relationships with the communities it serves.

Cabrillo College, so named in honor of Juan Rodriquez Cabrillo, a Portuguese explorer credited with the discovery of California in September 1542, found its own beginnings in October 1958. It was then that citizens of Santa Cruz and Monterey counties, living in the San Lorenzo, Santa Cruz, and Watsonville High School districts, approved formation of a junior college district.

The governing board, elected in January 1959, employed a staff to begin instruction in September of that year. More than 800 day and evening students enrolled in freshman classes in temporary quarters on the Watsonville High School campus; sophomores continued to attend neighboring junior colleges. The institution added sophomore classes to its program in September 1960.

The board of trustees, assisted by citizens' committees, selected the present site and worked hard to pass a $6.5-million bond issue in June 1960. Construction of the permanent campus began in 1961, and more than 2,000 students enrolled at the new facility in September 1962.

In April 1965 a $1.1-million bond issue was successfully passed that allowed for the construction of three additional college classroom wings. By the 1966 fall semester the wings were completed, and student capacity was increased to more than 5,000.

A second expansion of campus facilities, to the tune of $6 million, was made possible in 1973, when 20 acres of property adjoining the campus were purchased and three buildings of the occupational center were constructed. Programs housed in these facilities included construction trades, nursing, electronics, industrial technology, and early childhood education. Included in this acquisition was the historic Sesnon House, which is used for offices, as a site for community education classes, and as a community center enjoyed by numerous organizations throughout the year.

Today Cabrillo Community College stretches over 162 acres of hillside campus that overlooks the beautiful Monterey Bay. Its facilities include a college center, theater, library with microfilm references, bookstore, gymnasium, swimming pool, and stadium. The Watsonville Center features three classrooms and administrative offices in a convenient downtown location. Students participating in credit classes also benefit from services such as financial aid, career counseling, job placement, and student government activities.

In addition to two-year academic programs in arts and sciences, students can select from occupational training programs, including dental assisting, law enforcement, hazardous materials technology, and energy construction management.

As to the quality of education offered, suffice it to say that Cabrillo College is ranked number five out of the 107 public community colleges in the state in the rate of transfer to the University of California system.

Students pass in front of the administration building en route to their classes.

PATRONS

The following individuals, companies, and organizations have made a valuable commitment to the quality of this publication. Windsor Publications and the Santa Cruz Area Chamber of Commerce gratefully acknowledge their participation in Santa Cruz County: Restless Paradise.

Aliberti Construction Incorporated*
AMI Community Hospital of Santa Cruz*
Applied Geomechanics Incorporated
Beach Street Rick
Bed & Breakfast Innkeepers of Santa Cruz County*
Better Homes Realty-Howard Allen & Co.
Big Creek Lumber Company*
Cabrillo College*
Chaminade at Santa Cruz*
Chateau Des Fleurs
Citicorp Savings
Cowell College, UCSC—Faculty and Staff
Credit Bureau of Santa Cruz County*
J.J. Crosetti Co., Inc.*
Del Mar Foods*
Dominican Santa Cruz Hospital*
Ferranti Interdesign, Inc.
Filice Distributors*
Harry H. Fukutome Nursery*
Kaiser Sand & Gravel Company
Kitayama Brothers*
Ledyard Co.
Robert and Terry Locatelli Family
Marconi Civic Club
The Monterey Bay Natural-Historical Association
Monterey Mushrooms*
Naturipe Berry Growers*
Pacific Gas and Electric Company
Pajaro Valley Historical Association
Penniman Title Company*
Plantronics, Inc.*
The Railroads of F. Norman Clark*
REALTY WORLD-Nittler REALTORS
Rittenhouse Insurance Center*
Roses of Yesterday and Today*
Santa Cruz Seaside Company Boardwalk*
Sempervirens Fund
Richard A. Shaw, Inc., Frozen Foods*
Southwest Truck Service
Stained Glass Overlay
Tosello Enterprises, Inc.
Patricia Vomvolakis
Washington-Jensen & Associates, Architects & Engineers
Watsonville Area Chamber of Commerce & Agriculture*
Watsonville Community Hospital*
Watsonville Manor Residential Care Home
Watsonville Nurseries*
West Marine Products
Geo. H. Wilson, Inc.*
Wilson Brothers & Associates, Inc.*
Wyckoff, Richardson, Sanson, Allen and Locke-Paddon*

*Partners in Progress of Santa Cruz County: Restless Paradise. The histories of these companies and organizations appear in Chapter 7, beginning on page 95.

BIBLIOGRAPHY

NOTES

Several authors and their works deserve special notice in this bibliography. For further research, Donald Clark's *Santa Cruz County Place Names* will remain an invaluable reference work. Sandy Lydon's *Chinese Gold*, Henry Albert Willem van Coenen Torchiana's *History of the Mission Santa Cruz*, and Bette Lewis' works on Watsonville provide important insight in those specific subject areas. The monographs of Leon Roland, James Miller Guinn, Wallace Elliott, and E.S. Harrison enlighten early Santa Cruz County history, as they offer perspectives from a different era.

Margaret Koch's *Parade of the Past* is a particularly valuable companion to *Restless Paradise*. Her work represents a base from which all researchers begin their quest to find Santa Cruz County, for she has preserved portions of the area's history which might otherwise have been lost.

NEWSPAPER SOURCES

City On A Hill
Evening Pajaronian
The Mountain Echo
Santa Cruz Morning Sentinel
Santa Cruz Sentinel
Santa Cruz Surf
The Sun
Watsonville Morning-Sun
Watsonville Register-Pajaronian

OTHER SOURCES

Atkinson, Fred W. *100 Years in the Pajaro Valley (1769-1868)*. Watsonville: By the author, 1934.

Bancroft, Hubert Howe. *History of California*. 7 vols. San Francisco: The History Company, 1886.

Batman, Richard. *American Ecclesiastes*. New York: Harcourt Brace Jovanovich, 1984.

Batman, Richard. *The Outer Coast*. San Diego: Harcourt Brace Jovanovich, 1985.

Beck, Warren A., and Haase, Ynez D. *Historical Atlas of California*. Norman: University of Oklahoma Press, 1974.

Beechey, Frederick William. *Narrative of a Voyage to the Pacific and Beering's Strait*. London: Colburn and Bentley, 1831.

Birmingham, Stephen. *California Rich*. New York: Simon and Schuster, 1980.

Blumann, Ethel, and Thomas, Mabel W., eds. *California Local History; A Centennial Bibliography*. Stanford: Stanford University Press, 1950.

Bolton, Hubert Eugene. *Spanish Exploration in the Southwest, 1542-1706*. New York: Harper, 1916.

Chase, John. *The Sidewalk Companion to Santa Cruz Architecture*. Santa Cruz: Paper Vision Press, 1979.

City of Santa Cruz. City Planning Department. *Historic Preservation Plan*. Santa Cruz: City of Santa Cruz, 1974.

City of Santa Cruz. Historic Preservation Commission. *Santa Cruz Historic Building Survey*. San Francisco: Charles Hall Page and Associates, 1976.

Clark, Donald Thomas. *Santa Cruz County Place Names*. Santa Cruz: Santa Cruz Historical Society, 1986.

Clark, William B. *Gold Districts of California*. Sacramento: State of California, Division of Mines and Geology, 1963.

Cook, Sherburne F. *The Conflict Between the California Indian and White Civilization*. Berkeley: UC Press, 1976.

County Bank of Santa Cruz. *If Walls Could Talk*. Santa Cruz: County Bank, 1970.

Cowan, Robert Ernest. *Bibliography of the History of California and the Pacific West, 1510-1906*. San Francisco: Book Club of California, 1914.

Coy, Owen C. *California County Boundaries*. Berkeley: California Historical Survey Commission, 1923.

Coy, Owen C. *Guide to the County Archives of California*. Sacramento: State of California, Historical Survey Commission, 1919.

Deleissegues, Rebecca, and Mylar, Lucretia. *Early Days in Corralitos and Soquel*. Hollister: Evening Free Lance, 1929.

Delmatier, Royce D.; McIntosh, Clarence F.; and Waters, Earl G. *The Rumble of California Politics, 1848-1970*. New York: John Wiley and Sons, 1970.

Dillon, Richard, ed. *California Caravan: The 1846 Overland Trail Memoir of Margaret M. Heacox*. San Jose: Harlan-Young, 1966.

Donelly, Florence. "The San Lorenzo Paper Mill; Where the Redwoods Met the Sea." unpublished paper, n.d.

Dornin, May, and Pickerell, Albert G. *The University of California: A Pictorial History*. Berkeley: The Regents of the University of California, 1968.

Elliott, Wallace. *Illustrations... With Historical Sketch*. San Francisco: Wallace Elliott and Co., 1879.

Engelhardt, Father Zephyrin. *The Missions and Missionaries of California*. San Francisco: Barry, 1908-1915.

Farnham, Eliza Woodson. *California, In-Doors and Out*. New York: B. De Graaf, 1972.

Farquhar, Francis P., ed. *Up and Down California in 1860-1864; The Journal of William H. Brewer*. Berkeley: UC Press, 1966.

Fehliman, Clinton E. "Economic History of Santa Cruz County, California, 1850-1947." unpublished paper, University of California, Berkeley, 1947.

Fikes, Edith. "Santa Cruz County." unpublished paper, n.d.

Forbes, Alexander. *California...* London: Smith, Elder, 1839.

Forbes, Elizabeth. *Reminiscences of Seabright*. Seabright: By the author, 1915.

Francis, Phil. *Beautiful Santa Cruz County, California*. San Francisco: H.S. Crocker Co., 1896.

Fulcher, Edeline; Levy, Robert M.; and MacDonald, Susan L. "A History of the Wilder Ranch." unpublished paper, UCSC, 1970.

Gaudino, Riccardo. *A Day on the Bay, 1980*. Santa Cruz: City On A Hill Press, 1980.

Gibson, Ross Eric. *The Illustrated History of Lighthouse Point*. Santa Cruz: Gibsonian Arts, 1982.

Gilbert, Benjamin F., and Melendy, Brett H. *The Governors of California*. Georgetown, California: The Talisman Press, 1965.

Greenlee, Jason. "Vegetation, Fire History and Fire Potential of Big Basin Redwoods State Park, California." unpublished Ph.D. thesis, UCSC, 1983.

Gudnason, Kay. *Rings in the Redwoods*. Mount Hermon: Mount Hermon Association, 1972.

Guest, Florion. "The Establishment of the Villa de Branciforte." *California Historical Society Quarterly*, March 1962.

Guinn, James Miller. *History of the State of California and Biographic Record of Santa Cruz, San Benito, Monterey and San Luis Obispo Counties*. Chicago: Chapman Publishing, 1903.

Harrison, Edward. *History of Santa Cruz County*. Oakland: Pacific Press, 1892.

Heizer, Robert F., ed. *California Indians*. Vol. VIII of the *Handbook of North American Indians*. Edited by William C. Sturtevant. 20 vols. Washington, D.C.: Smithsonian Institution, 1978.

Heizer, Robert F., ed. *The Costanoan Indians*. Cupertino: California History Center, 1974.

Heizer, Robert F., and Whipple, M.A. *The California Indians*. Berkeley: UC Press, 1951.

Hittell, John S. *Hittell's Hand-Book of Pacific Coast Travel*. San Francisco: A.L. Bancroft and Company, 1895.

Hoffman, Ogden. *Reports of Land Cases De-*

termined in the U.S. District Court for the Northern District of California, June Term, 1853 to June Term, 1858. Vol. I. San Francisco: Hubert, 1862.

Hogue, Harland E., and Patton, Carl S. *A Century of Christian Witness; History of the First Congregational Church, Santa Cruz, California.* Santa Cruz: First Congregational Church, 1963.

Hoover, Mildred Brooke; Rensch, Hero Eugene; and Rensch, Ethel Grace. *Historic Spots in California.* Stanford: Stanford University Press, 1966.

Jensen, Kenneth. "The Lime Industry in Santa Cruz County." unpublished paper, 1976.

Johnson, Viola, ed. *The Watsonville Band, California's Most Honored Marching Band; The First 25 Years.* Watsonville: Pajaro Press, 1972.

Kaye, Michael S. *The Teacher Was the Sea; The Story of Pacific High School.* New York: Links Publishing, 1972.

Kimbro, Edna; Ryan, Mary Ellen; Jackson, Robert H.; Milliken, Randall; and Neuerburg, Norman. *Restoration Research, Santa Cruz Mission Adobe, Santa Cruz Mission S.H.P.* Davenport: Historical Investigations, 1985.

Koch, Margaret. *Santa Cruz County; Parade of the Past.* Fresno: Valley Publishers, 1973.

Koch, Margaret. *They Called It Home.* Santa Cruz: Valley Publishers, 1974.

Koch, Margaret. *Yesterday, Today and Tomorrow.* Santa Cruz: Wilson Bros. and Associates, 1964.

Kroeber, A.L. *Handbook of the Indians of California.* New York: Dover Publications, 1976.

LeBoeuf, Burney, and Kaza, Stephanie. *The Natural History of Ano Nuevo.* Pacific Grove: Boxwood Press, 1981.

Legner, Mary, compiler. "Evergreen Cemetery." unpublished paper, 1980.

Lewis, Betty. *Highlights in the History of Watsonville, California.* Watsonville: Watsonville Federal Savings, 1975.

Lewis, Betty. *Watsonville; Memories That Linger.* Vol. II. Santa Cruz: Valley Publishers, 1980.

Lewis, Betty. *Watsonville Yesterday.* Watsonville: Mehl's Colonial Chapel, 1978.

Lydon, Sandy. *Chinese Gold.* Capitola: Capitola Book Company, 1985.

Lydon, Sandy, and Swift, Carolyn. *Soquel Landing to Capitola-by-the-Sea.* Cupertino: California History Center, 1978.

McCaleb, Charles S. *Surf, Sand and Streetcars.* Glendale: Interurbans, 1977.

McEnery, Thomas, ed. *California Cavalier; The Journal of Captain Thomas Fallon.* San Jose: Inishfallen Enterprises, 1978.

McHaley, Gertrude. "History of Santa Cruz County." unpublished paper, n.d.

McWilliams, Carey. *Factories in the Field.* Santa Barbara: Peregrine Publishers, 1971.

Margolin, Malcolm. *The Ohlone Way.* Berkeley: Heyday Books, 1978.

Marion, Homer. "Santa Cruz County Resources." unpublished paper, 1963.

Mathes, W. Michael. *Vizcaino and Spanish Expansion in the Pacific Ocean, 1580-1630.* San Francisco: California Historical Society, 1968.

Mora, Jo. *Californios.* New York: Doubleday, 1949.

Nakane, Kazuko. *Nothing Left in My Hands.* Seattle: Young Pine Press, 1985.

O'Brien, Frederick. "The Land of Lotus—Capitola." *Sunset Magazine,* II (August 1903): 340-344.

Olin, L.G. "The Development and Promotion of Santa Cruz Tourism." unpublished M.A. thesis, San Jose State College, n.d.

Parish, Narcissa Louise. *The Early History of the Santa Cruz Region.* unpublished M.A. thesis, University of California, Berkeley, 1924.

Patten, Phyllis Bertorelli. *Oh, That Reminds Me . . .* Felton: Big Trees Press, 1969.

Patten, Phyllis Bertorelli. *Santa Cruz Mission: La Exaltacion de la Santa Cruz.* Santa Cruz: By the author, 1974.

Pattie, James O. *The Personal Narrative of James O. Pattie.* New York: Lippincott, 1962.

Payne, Stephen. *A Howling Wilderness; A History of the Summit Road Area of the Santa Cruz Mountains.* Cupertino: California History Center, 1978.

Perry, Frank. *Lighthouse Point: Reflections on Monterey Bay History.* Soquel: GBH Publishing, 1982.

Pfremmer, Patricia. *Santa Cruz, 1850-1976; A Selective Bibliography Based on Resources in the University of California, Santa Cruz.* Santa Cruz: UCSC, 1976.

Phister, Colonal Fred. *The National Guardsman in Camp . . . Camp Stoneman, Santa Cruz, August 15 to August 23, 1885.* Sacramento: State Printer, 1885

Pratt, Julius W. *Expansionists of 1898.* Baltimore: The Johns Hopkins Press, 1936.

Raymond, I.H. *Santa Cruz County; Resources, Advantages, Objects of Interests.* Santa Cruz: Santa Cruz Development Association, 1887.

Reid, Robert Morrison. "Route of the Portola Expedition, 1769." Santa Cruz: published paper, n.d.

Reihhardt, Richard. "A Retrospective Look at Some of Northern California's Favorite Summer Resorts, 1871-1920." *San Francisco,* VII (July 1965): 24-29; 40-41.

Reinstedt, Randall A. *Portraits of the Past.* Monterey: Monterey Savings and Loan Association, 1979.

Reinstedt, Randall A. *Shipwrecks and Sea Monsters of California's Central Coast.* Carmel: Ghost Town Publications, 1975.

Rose, Kenneth D. "Wettest in the West: San Francisco and Prohibition in 1924." *California History,* LXV (December 1986: 284-296.

Rowland, Leon. *Annals of Santa Cruz.* Santa Cruz: By the author, n.d.

Rowland, Leon. *Villa de Branciforte.* Santa Cruz: By the author, 1941.

Santa Cruz Board of Trade. *The City of Santa Cruz and Vicinity, California.* San Francisco: Murdock Press, 1905.

Santa Cruz, California, General Plan. Santa Cruz: City of Santa Cruz, 1962.

Santa Cruz Chamber of Commerce. *The Industrial Future of Santa Cruz.* San Francisco: Industrial Survey Associates, 1953.

Santa Cruz County. Soil Conservation Service. *Santa Cruz County Resources.* Santa Cruz: Santa Cruz County, 1963.

Santa Cruz Historical Society. *News and Notes.* Nos. 1-40, October 1954-June 1968.

Simpson, Lesley Byrd. *Branciforte.* San Francisco: Harry W. Porte, 1935.

Southern Pacific Company. *Resorts Along the Coast Line and in the Santa Cruz Mountains.* San Francisco: Southern Pacific Company (1903?).

Souza, Margaret Ann. "The History of the Santa Cruz Public Library System." unpublished thesis, San Jose State College, 1970.

State of California. Department of Parks and Recreation. *Santa Cruz Mission SHP Preliminary General Plan.* Sacramento: State Printing Office, 1984.

State of California. Disaster Office. *The Big Flood: California, 1955.* Sacramento: State Printing Office, 1956.

Sullivan, Charles. *Like Modern Edens.* Cupertino: California History Center, 1982.

Taylor, Paul. *On the Ground in the Thirties.* Salt Lake City: Peregrine Smith Books, 1983.

Thomas, John Hunter. *Flora of the Santa Cruz Mountains of California.* Stanford: Stanford University Press, 1961.

Torchiana, H.A. van Coenen. *Story of the Mission Santa Cruz.* San Francisco: Paul Elder and Company, 1933.

U.S. Congress. House. *Executive Documents.* Appendix II (Foreign Relations of the United States, 1894, Affairs In Hawaii), 53d Cong., 3d sess., 1895.

U.S. Department of Commerce. Bureau of the Census. *U.S. Census of Population: 1850, 1860, 1870, and 1880.*

U.S. Geological Survey. *Geological Atlas of the U.S.: Santa Cruz Folio, 1909.* No city, n.d.

U.S. Works Progress Administration. Federal Writers' Project. *The WPA Guide to California.* New York: Pantheon Books, 1984 (reprint of 1939 work).

UCSC Environmental Studies Board. *Pacific Garden Mall.* Santa Cruz, UCSC, 1974.

Valle, Rosemary K. "James Ohio Pattie and the 1927-28 Alta California Measles Epidemic." *California Historical Quarterly,* LII (Spring 1973): 28-36.

Verardo, Denzil. *Big Basin.* Los Altos: Sempervirens Fund, 1973.

Verardo, Denzil and Jennie. "Echos." *The Mountain Echo,* 1974-present.

Verardo, Denzil and Jennie. *Short Historic Tours of Big Basin Redwoods State Park.* Los Altos: Sempervirens Fund and the Santa Cruz Mountains Natural History Association, 1974.

Verardo, Jennie. "The Mountain Echo: Notes on the Acquisition of Big Basin Redwoods State Park." unpublished research report for the Sempervirens Fund, 1973.

Warrick, Sheridan F., ed. *The Natural History of the UCSC Campus.* Santa Cruz: UCSC Environmental Field Program, 1982.

Watkins, Rolin G. *History of Monterey and Santa Cruz Counties, California.* 2 vols. Chicago: S.J. Clarke Publishing Company, 1925.

Watsonville Buddhist Church. *60th Anniversary 1906-66; Build a Greater Sangha.* Watsonville: Watsonville Buddhist Church, 1966.

Watsonville Register-Pajaronian. *Watsonville: The First Hundred Years.* Watsonville: Watsonville Chamber of Commerce, 1952.

Webber, Burt. *Retaliation: Japanese Attacks and Allied Countermeasures on the Pacific Coast in WWII.* Corvallis, Oregon: Oregon State University Press, 1975.

Wycoff, Hubert. *Memories of the Pajaro Valley: An Interview with Edward Porter Pfingst.* Watsonville: Pajaro Valley Historical Association, 1973.

Yamamoto, Carol. "The Watsonville Filipino Race Riots." unpublished paper, Cabrillo College, 1973.

INDEX

PARTNERS IN PROGRESS INDEX

Aliberti Construction Incorporated, 125
AMI Community Hospital of Santa Cruz, 118-119
Bed & Breakfast Innkeepers of Santa Cruz County, 134-135
Big Creek Lumber Company, 110-111
Cabrillo College, 138
Chaminade at Santa Cruz, 136-137
Credit Bureau of Santa Cruz County, 124
Crosetti Co., Inc., J.J., 116
Del Mar Foods, 114-115
Dominican Santa Cruz Hospital, 127
Filice Distributors, 117
Fukutome Nursery, Harry H., 97
Kitayama Brothers, 102-103
Monterey Mushrooms, 106-107
Naturipe Berry Growers, 108
Penniman Title Company, 130
Plantronics, Inc., 128-129
Railroads of F. Norman Clark, The, 120-121
Rittenhouse Insurance Center, 132-133
Roses of Yesterday and Today, 112-113
Santa Cruz Area Chamber of Commerce, 96
Santa Cruz Seaside Company Boardwalk, 98-99
Shaw, Inc., Frozen Foods, Richard A., 104-105
Watsonville Area Chamber of Commerce & Agriculture, 126
Watsonville Community Hospital, 109
Watsonville Nurseries, 100
Wilson, Inc., Geo. H., 122-123
Wilson Brothers & Associates, Inc., 131
Wyckoff, Richardson, Sanson, Allen and Locke-Paddon, 101

GENERAL INDEX
Italicized numbers indicate illustrations.

Abbott, Chuck and Esther, 87-89
Abbott, Mark, 89
Adams, Clara, 43
Agriculture, 50-51, *51, 52, 60, 61,* 68-69, 71
Alcalde system, 35-36
All Souls Unitarian Church, *34-35*
Alvarado, Juan Bautista, 17-18
Alzina, Francisco, 37
Amat, Thaddeus, 37, 38
American Anti-Saloon League, 80
Anthony, Elihu, 23, 25-26, 38
Anthony, Susan B., 76
Apple Annual, *70, 71*
Aptos, 67-68
Aptos Hotel, 68
Aptos Militia, 81
Arano, José, 67-68
Asesara, Lorenzo, 14
Ashly, Delos, 41
Baird, John H., 24
Baldwin, Levi K., 51
Baldwin and Wilder Dairy, 51
Ball, Bessie and Lucy, *28*

Bancroft, Herbert Howe, 19
Bates, Joel, 66
Bear Flag Revolt, 19
Bell, Thomas L., 56
Ben Lomond, 55-57, *55*
Ben Lomond School, *44*
Ben Lomond Winery, 56, 65
Bennett, Eben, 65
Bennett, Jackson and Winston, 55
Bierce, Ambrose, 74
Big Basin Mercantile Company, 55
Big Basin State Park, 29, *52,* 91
Big Creek Power Company, 31
Billings, F.W., 56
Blackburn, William, 35-36, 37
Blasting powder industry, 24-25
Bolcoff, José Antonio, 22
Bolcoff adobe, *88*
Borica, Governor Diégo de, 16, 17
Bouchard, Hippolyte de, 17
Boulder Creek, 52, *53,* 55, *61,* 65
Boulder Creek School District, 52
Branciforte, Marques de, 16
Branciforte, Villa de, *8-9,* 16-17, *16,* 21
Brookdale Lodge, *54*
Brown, James and Peter, 24
Buelna, Commisionado Joaquin, 17
Burns, Thomas, 56
Cabrillo, Juan Rodriquez, 11
Cabrillo Community College, 44
Cahoon, Benjamin, 66
California Powder Works, 24-25
California Sugar Beet Company, 66
California Sugar Refinery, 69
Camp McQuaide, 81
Capitola, 26, 31, *58,* 66-67, *66, 67*
Capitola Hotel, *48-49*
Carousel, 90
Carr, Jesse D., 68
Casa del Rey Hotel, 33
Case, Mary, 43
Castle Rock State Park, 91
Castro, Maria de los Angeles, 22
Catholic churches, *36-37*
Cement industry, 50, 77-78
Charles III, 12
Chestnutwood, J.A., 44
Chestnutwood's Business College, 44, *45*
Chinese Christian Society, 38
Chinese immigrants, 38, 40
Church, Thomas, 47
City Street Improvement Company, *24-25*
Civilian Conservation Corps, 81
Clark, Dr. H.H., 31
Coast Dairies and Land Company, 50
Collins, George, 91
Conservation Associates, 91
Coope, J.F., 29, 56, 65
Cooper, Captain John, 37, 68
Cooper, William, 37
Cooper House, 37, 84
Costanoans, 11, 14, 17; basketry, *11*
Costanso, Miguel, 13
Cowell, Henry, 23, *23*
Cowell, Mrs. Henry, *23*
Cowell Lime and Cement Company, 23, 77-78
Cowell Redwoods State Park, 23
Cowell Wharf, *24-25*
Crespi, Padre, *12*

Danbenbiss, John, 66
Davenport, Captain John Pope, 49, 50, *50*
Davenport, Mrs. John, *50*
Davenport Landing, 49-50
Davis, Isaac E., 23
Dudley, William, 29
Earthquakes, 77-78
East Side Methodist Episcopal Church, *38*
Ellsworth, John, 52
Fallon, Thomas, 37
Felton, 65
Filipinos, 80
Fire management, 11, *11*
Fisk, George H., 29
Floods, 77, 86, *86, 87*
Flour production, 22-23
Ford, Charles, 69, 71
Ford Company, 69
Ford's Department Store, 69
Free library, *42*
Fremont, John C., 19; exploring party, *18*
Gaffey, William, 71
Gage, Governor Henry T., 29, *30,* 77
Garfield Park, 39
Garfield Park Tabernacle, *39*
Geology, 9, 11
Giant Dipper roller coaster, 33, *63,* 90
Gillette, James, 76
Government Center, 86
Graham, Isaac, 17-19
Graham vs. Charles Roussilan, 36
Grand Central Hotel, 65
Grant School, *43*
Great Depression, 80
Great White Fleet, 78-79, *79*
Guerra, Commandante José, 16
Haight, Lansing, 66
Hames, John, 66
Hammond, Gervis, 66
Harte, Bret, 73
Heath, Frank, 75
Hicks, Achilles Scipio and Napoleon Bonaparte, 56
"Highways 4 and 100" issue, 87
Hihn, Frederick A., 26, *27,* 66-67, 71
Hill, Andrew P., 27, *28,* 29, 75
Hinckley, Roger, 66
Historical preservation, 87-89
Historic Preservation Commission, 89
Holmes Lime Kiln Company, 23
Holy Cross School, 44
Hoover, Theodore, 51-52
Houston, James D., 74
Howden Castle, *56*
Hutchings, Moses, 71
Indians. *See* Costanoans.
IXL Company, 23
Japanese, 39, 83
Jeter, William T., 75-76, *76*
Jimeño, Manuel, 17
Johnston, Adam, 14
Jones, Mrs. S.A., 29
Jordan, Albion P., 23
Joss House, *39*
Judicial system, 35-36
Kenna, Father Robert, *30*
King, Howard, 91
King, John, 49
Kirby, Georgianna Bruce, 74

143

Kirby, Gershal, 66
Knight, Benjamin, 75
Kooser, R.S., 29
Kron, Jacob, 22
Kron Tanning Company, 21-22
Labor strikes, 80-81
Lampier, Faye, *78*
Lasuen, Father, 13
Laurel School, *42*
Leibbrandt's Bathhouses, *5*, 31
Leonard, Doris, 91
Lick, James, 47
Lick Observatory, 47
Lighthouse Field, 87
Lighthouse Point, 89
Lime industry, *22-23*, 23, 77-78
Lodge, Michael and Martina Castro, 66
Loma Prieta Lumber Company, *26*
Look, Claude A. "Tony," *90*, 91
Lorenson, Edward, 79
Lorenzo, 52, 55
Love, Captain Harry, 55
Lumber industry, 26-27, 50, 52, 66
McCall, Hugh, 66
McCrackin, Josephine Clifford, 27, *29*, 73-74, *74*
McCulloch-Hartnell, 14
McElroy, John, 41
McHenry, Dean, 47
McHugh and Bianchi building, *88*, 89
McPherson, Duncan, 40, 76
McPherson, Fred D., 40
Madrone Villa, *54*
Majors, Joseph, 19, 22-23
Martinelli, Stephen, 68
Martinelli's Cider and Soda Works, 68
Menasco, James S., 69
Methodist Episcopal Church (Watsonville), *38*
Methodist North and South churches, 38
Micheltorena, Manuel, 18
Middleton, Henry L., 29, 55
Miller's Neptune Baths, *5*, 31
Mission Santa Cruz, *8-9*, 13-14, *15*, 17, *17*
Morey, A.A., 69
Moroto Investment Company, 51
Mount McAbee, 91
Mount Hermon Association, 39
Mountain Echo, 41
Municipal wharf, *82*
National Guard Company L, *72-73*, 79
Native Sons of the Golden West Convention, *75*
Newspapers, 40-41, 43
Ocean Shore Railroad, 50
Ocean View Hotel, 50
O'Neill, Edward and Frank, 24
O'Neill, Jack, 90
Opera House, 75
Ortega, Sergeant, *12*
Otto, Ernest, *40*
Overland, 73
Pacific Avenue, *80*, 88-89, *88, 94-95*
Pacific Garden Mall, 89
Pacific Gas and Electric Company, 89
Pacific Manufacturing Company, 56
Pacific Mills School, 56
Pacific Ocean House, 31
Packard, John Q., 29, 56
Pajaro River, *12*, 13

Pajaro Valley Orphan Asylum, 38
Pajaro Valley Railroad, 71
Palo Alto, 66-67
Palou, Father Francisco, 13
Paper production, 23-24
Pardee, Governor George, 76
Peckham, Judge, 68
Peery, Joseph W., 52
Penny Press, 41
Peralta, Luis, 13
Peyton, Bernard and William C., 25
Pierce, James, 56
Pope House, 31
Porter, C.K. and B.F., 66
Porter, Warren, 76
Portland Cement Company, *50-51*
Portolá, Don Gaspar de, 12-13, *12*
Prewett, John, 22
Priest, James, 56
Private Revitalization of Downtown, 88-89
Prohibition, 80
Public Works Administration, 81
Quintana, Father Andres, 14
Railroad Wharf, *24-25*
Rancho del Oso, 51-52
Rancho Salsipuedes, 17
Ratcliffe, W.R., 71
Reagan, Ronald, *92*
Red Line, 26
Redwood preservation, 27, 29, 52-53, 55, 91
Reed, Charles Wesley, 29
Register-Pajaronian, 40
Republican State Convention (1906), 76
Retreats, 39-40
Rice, David, 68
Richards, Judge John, 27
Richards, W.W., 29, *33*
Rickel, James Jr., 83
Riley, Joseph, 22
Rodger, Winfield Scott, 41, *42*
Roosevelt, President Theodore, 76, *78-79*
Roxas, Justiniano, *14*
Sailing, *57*
St. Charles Hotel, 31
St. Francis School of Watsonville, 38
St. Patrick's Catholic Church, 37-38
Sal, Don Hermenegildo, 13
Salz Tannery, A.K., 22
Sanborn, Lucius, 69
San Lorenzo Flume, *20-21*, 27
San Lorenzo Flume and Lumber Company, 27
San Lorenzo River, 13
Santa Clara Turnpike Company, 26, 66
Santa Cruz (steamship), 23
Santa Cruz and Felton Railroad, 27
Santa Cruz Art League, 75
Santa Cruz Beach Company, 32
Santa Cruz Beach Cottage and Tent City Corporation, 31-32, *33*
Santa Cruz Boardwalk, *32, 63*, 90
Santa Cruz, Capitola and Watsonville Railway, 67
Santa Cruz Congregational Church, 38
Santa Cruz County Courthouse, *36*
Santa Cruz County Hall of Records, *36*
Santa Cruz, Garfield Park and Capitola Electric Railway Company, 31
Santa Cruz High School, 44
Santa Cruz Light and Power Company, 31

Santa Cruz Lighthouse, *3*, *59*
Santa Cruz Portland Cement Company, 50
Santa Cruz Railroad, 26
Santa Cruz Surfing Club, 90
Santa Cruz-Watsonville Railroad, 68
Santa Maria del Mar, 39
Save Lighthouse Point Association, 87
Scotts Valley, 65
Seacliff State Beach, *90*
Seaside, 50
Sempervirens Club, *28*, 29
Sempervirens Fund, *90*, 91
Sentinel, 41, 76; newsroom, *40*
Serra, Father Junípero, 12-13
Shelby, John, 66
Silver Lumber Mills, 52
Skyline-to-the-Sea Trail, 91
Smith, James P., 31
Smith, Page, 74
Solá, Governor Pablo Vicente, 17
Soquel, 66-67
Southern Pacific Coast Railroad, 27, 52, 55, 65, 69
Spreckels, Claus, 26, 69, 71
Stowe, William W., 75
"Suntan Special," 90
Surf, 41
Surfing, *58*, 90
Surfing Museum, 89, 90
Swanton, Fred Willer, 29, 31-33
Swanton Beach Park, 33
Swanton Investment Company, 33
Sweet, Paul, 19
Tanning industry, 21-22, 66
Taylor, A.A., 41, *41*
Taylor, the Reverend William, 38
Torchiana, H.A. Van Coenen, 74
Trousset, Leon, 75
Twin Lakes, 39
University of California, Santa Cruz, 41, 43, *46*, 47, *62, 92-93*, 93
Valencia Mill, 26
Valkenburgh, Henry Van, 23-24
Varian, Dorothy, *90*, 91
Varian, Russell, 91
Veteran's Memorial Building, *82*
Vizcaíno, Sebastián, 11-12
Waddell, William, 50
Walden, Max, 89
Walker, Chief of Police William, *81*
Walter, Carrie Stevens, 29
Waters, James, 68
Watson, Judge John H., 43
Watsonville, 68-69
Watsonville Airport, 81
Watsonville High School, 44
Watsonville Mill and Lumber Company, 69
Watsonville Naval Air Station, 81
Weeks, William, 75
White, William, 68
Wilder, Delos D., 51
Wilder Ranch, 51, 81
Williams, Isaac, 68
Willson, I.C., 56
Wing, Colonel, 29
Woman's Christian Temperance Union, *53*, 80
Works Progress Administration, 81
World War I, 79
World War II, 81